WALKS
WEST DO

GW00580055

20 fully detailed country walks
of moderate length along
public rights of way
through some of the
finest scenery in England

Rodney Legg

DORSET PUBLISHING COMPANY
WINCANTON PRESS, NATIONAL SCHOOL
NORTH STREET, WINCANTON, SOMERSET BA9 9AT

Dorset area distribution
by Maurice Hann, 36 Langdon Road,
Parkstone, Poole, Dorset BH14 9EH
telephone (0202) 738248

Also by Rodney Legg

Publishing details. Second, revised edition 1991
Copyright Rodney Legg © 1986–91
Printed in Great Britain at the Alden Press, Oxford

International standard book number
[ISBN] 0 902129 73 2

Contents

THE ROUTES —
AND FOREWARNINGS!

ALL ROUTES in this book are along public rights of way — footpaths, bridleways, byways, or unclassified publicly-maintained roads. Here and there the latter include sections of tarred public roads but such stretches are kept to a minimim, being included only where they are necessary to complete a circuit. There are also some permissive paths, such as around Golden Cap, where there is a general right of access across an open space.

The walks have already been tested on readers of the Dorset County Magazine and their suggestions incorporated.

Allow at least an additional twenty-five per cent to our mileage estimates — it is impossible to walk a straight line in the countryside.

Remember that these walks tended to be researched in conditions that were generally average to good, and described in the state in which we found them. Only you can judge the current weather conditions, and choose your footwear accordingly. Some meadowland still floods in winter. A path we might have encountered in extreme drought can be very different after the wettest July of the century.

Allow also for the fact that here and there the odd hedge will have been grubbed and other landmarks may have appeared. This is being written at a time when diversification away from traditional agriculture has led to a spate of planning applications for golf courses. Leisure and fishing lakes have also started to appear. Every barn now has its yuppies. Many paths are in the process of being legally diverted, often to remove them from farmyards or the immediate vicinity of people's homes. An additional element of confusion is that public houses are being renamed for something trendier — such as the Woolmington Hotel at Sherborne which has become The Pageant and the Three Boars at Lydlinch which is now the Deer Park.

Detour around any unlawful obstructions and report them to the Rights of Way Office, Dorset County Council, County Hall, Dorchester. Don't let such things spoil your day — the only cure for a blocked path is to use it. May the delights of some of the finest mixes of scenery and seascapes in England make up for any shortcomings that you encounter.

Lyme Regis undercliff and river

Distance: 5 miles.
Difficult bits: One – a steep climb out of the undercliff.
State of paths: Otherwise good; easy to find.
Scenery: Chimney Rock outcrop and views of Lyme's coast.
Historical interest: Grotto at Lepers Well; Lyme's Museum; mediaeval Cobb Harbour; beach where the Duke of Monmouth landed in 1685.
Natural history: Undercliff National Nature Reserve; badger sets; dippers on the River Lim.
Literary associations: Jane Austen's *Persuasion*, John Fowles's *French Lieutenant's Woman*.

LYME REGIS has the sort of compacted landscape that gives a five mile walk like this far more appeal and interest than you could normally cram into a short distance. Apart from sampling the wilderness region of cliff-edge landslips, and skirting inland to some quiet countryside, the walk also encircles the town centre at Lyme but without degenerating into something unacceptably urban.

For you can walk in solitude through the middle of Lyme to the sea, following the fast-flowing River Lim, and watch dippers and grey wagtails in the heart of the town. Because this is a short walk, with so many bonus points, it is worth spending longer than usual in the time that may be involved in driving to the start. From Bournemouth to Lyme, for example, is fifty miles, but the walk does repay the drive.

Drive through the centre of Lyme Regis along the town's main street, climbing uphill along the road signposted "A 3052, Exeter". Towards the top of the very long, steep hill there is a sign pointing left to "The Cobb". Immediately after this junction, also on the left, is a large carpark.

It has blue notices: "Long-stay carpark". Leave the carpark at the opposite end from the entrance. The tarred area becomes narrower and you are funnelled into a track, with a line of pine trees, between the gardens of houses and bungalows.

At the end of the track is a signpost "Footpath to Ware" and you turn right. Go through the gate into the field, but then turn to the left, keeping close to the scrubland. After about 50 yards you cross a small stream and go through another iron gate.

In this field you keep to the right-hand side, climbing a slope signposted "Coast Path". At the top you go through another gate. To the left

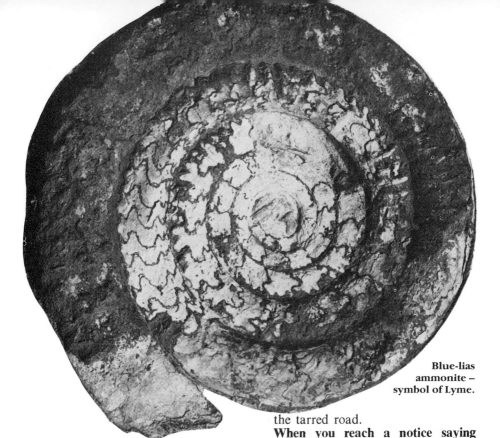

**Blue-lias
ammonite –
symbol of Lyme.**

the tarred road.

When you reach a notice saying "Underhill Farm" you stop and turn immediately right, beside an electricity pole marked "Underhill Farm 2325". A second public path leaves the main path at this point. After having deviated slightly to the right, you climb directly uphill, at ninety degrees to the main track, and climb the principal outcrop in front of you. On the northern side of this summit, amongst the dense sycamores, there is a popular badger lavatory, with more than a dozen examples of recent use.

A prominent path runs downhill, inland, but to the left of it—across the lavatory—there is a second path, and this is the one you want. Take this, with your back directly towards the sea. You pass to the right of a moss and spindle-covered rocky out-

of this there is a green seat with a view over the Cobb harbour and the shingle beach where the Duke of Monmouth landed in 1685. The next section of the path passes badger sets and is at the top of a noticeably landslipped cliff though this, by Lyme standards, is only modest subsidence.

At the end of this stretch there is a wooden gate into a small field. Walk across to the wooden bungalow, Clifden, and leave the field by the small kissing gate.

You now turn left along the tarred road, and keep on the road across a rougher section, to a second length of tar where there is a notice that you are in the Undercliff National Nature Reserve. The public path continues into the reserve along

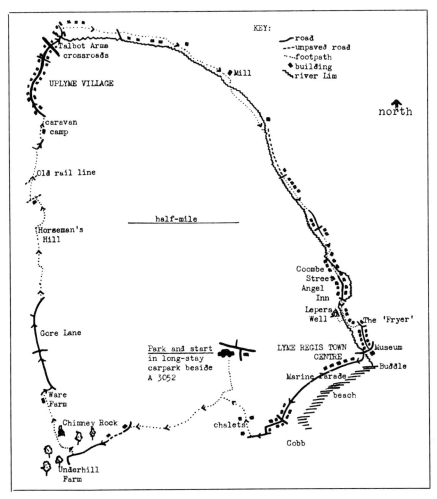

KEY:
road
unpaved road
footpath
building
river Lim

Talbot Arms crossroads

UPLYME VILLAGE

Mill

north

caravan camp

Old rail line

half-mile

Horseman's Hill

Coombe Street
Angel Inn
Lepers Well

The 'Fryer'

Gore Lane

Park and start in long-stay carpark beside A 3052

LYME REGIS TOWN CENTRE

Museum

Buddle

Marine Parade

beach

Ware Farm

Chimney Rock

chalets

Cobb

Underhill Farm

crop and then go downhill across a narrow valley at the foot of the main cliff. The badgers conveniently keep open the course of the public path, scraping an easily followed track through the vegetation.

As you near the top, stop and look upwards to your right. Surmounting a twenty-foot outcrop of ivy-clad rock there is a pillar of stone. This is Chimney Rock which, in a more romantic age, was a popular beauty spot for Victorian and Edwardian Lyme. The natural limestone pillar, its surface eaten by water into masses of cup-like depressions, is like the hoar-stones of the Rollrights in Oxfordshire. It stands 11 feet high, and all round the base are the eroding initials of 19th century visitors.

At the top of the cliff, just above Chimney Rock, there is a field and farmhouse. Duck under the wire and walk straight across the field to the black-painted gate immediately beside the house. The public path crosses the garden of Ware Farm and emerges on to a tarred road.

Turn right along the road and walk downhill to the junction with a second lane. Turn left here and walk uphill for about 200 yards to the main road.

Cross over, and walk along Gore Lane, which is signposted to Uplyme. Continue straight ahead past the turning to Hill Farm. About 120 yards further on there is a passing place on the left side of the road. This leads into a recessed gateway, with an iron gate at the end and a glimpse of Uplyme church.

Go through this gate and keep the main left-hand field hedge directly to your left. After a short distance this boundary becomes a stretch of iron railings, leading to a kink in the fence where concrete fencing posts take over. You slip through the fence at the kink and continue straight ahead, keeping the concrete fencing to your right. At the far corner of the field, on the top of Horseman's Hill, you slip through the wire and turn to your right for four paces, to the remains of an iron stile at the top of a deep-cut footpath.

This track runs between a field bank and a garden wall, and leads downhill to a flight of steps beside the garage of the house (No. 1 Cuckoo Hill). Turn left, along the tarred road, and pass the main front of the house. Just after the end of the house, on the right, there is a wooden stile and a "Public footpath" sign. Cross into this field and turn to the right, diagonally across it, and over another two stiles that takes you across the track of the Axminster to Lyme Regis railway.

Turn right and walk diagonally across the next field, downhill, head-ing towards Uplyme church. You cross a stream, go through a gate, and walk up a tarred track. You keep immediately to the left of the camp shop, and follow the public path beside the buildings to the entrance of Hook Farm caravan park.

Turn left on to the tarred road and walk downhill. Go straight over at the crossroads, following the Axminster signpost. You come out on the main road at the Talbot Arms and cross over into Church Street. This takes you over a bridge, crossing the River Lim, and you pass a row of three cottages on your right.

Just after the last, called Brook Cottage, there is a public footpath signposted to the right. Take this path, which is in part surrounded by garlic and passes above an attractive bend in the river. Cross over the next road, into Mill Lane which has a sign: "Public footpath to Lyme Regis". One section of this path has slipped towards the river, but is still firm enough to walk. The path passes close to the wooden water-wheel at the mill and then crosses a footbridge.

A little further downstream you pass a waterfall and then re-cross the river. Follow the track along the river towards the sea. You continue straight ahead across a tarred road, beside a deep-arched bridge, on to a riverside path that is now tarred and formal. After Higher Mill another road is crossed, and the next section of the walk passes a house called Lymbrook where the river surges around a sharp bend.

You come to Mill Green and Coombe Street where, opposite the Angel Inn, is the start of another section of riverside path. The river here is at two levels, the path

Edwardian ladies on the footbridge below the mill.

running between them. At one point an attractive but modern stone bridge (misleadingly back-dated

Georgian ladies skinny-dipping at Lyme Regis: Cruikshank's 'Hydromania', 1819.

with a stone saying "774 AD") leads across to a small public garden around the Lepers Well. The water trickles into a trough in a grotto: "Near this spot some 700 years ago a hospital for lepers was dedicated to St Mary and the Holy Spirit."

The path comes out on a main

The path passes beside the mill wheel [behind the rear bike wheel].

street at "The Fryer" fish and chip shop. Turn right, along Coombe Street, which emerges in Bridge Street beside the Philpot Museum. Its curator is John Fowles, author of *The French Lieutenant's Woman*, who lives in Belmont, the Coadestone mansion at the top of Cobb Road.

Cross the mouth of the Lyme, called the Buddle, and turn left immediately after the bus-stop. Walk along Marine Parade, passing the ostentatious 18th century lead drainpipes on Library Cottage. Cross the road leading into the Cobb and continue along Ozone Terrace.

Don't believe anything you read about Jane Austen staying in a house called Wings (demolished 1945) which stood beside the Marine Parade, on her 1803-04 visits to Lyme – it wasn't even built at the time!

Turn left at the end, beside the public lavatories, and then turn right along the seafront. Turn right abruptly on the other side of the bowling green and walk up a flight of steps beside the chalet No 12, called "Cobb View". The path continues straight ahead uphill, passing to the left of chalet number 24. At the top of the steps you cross a stile and walk into a field.

Turn to your right and then go through the gate. The next gate, on the left, takes you back into the carpark. □

Thorncombe and Forde Abbey

Distance: 7 miles.

Difficult bits: One or two fences without stiles, and finding your bearings in a dense wood, but you are soon out of it.

State of paths: Generally damp.

Scenery: Undulating land of small woods, pastures and fruit farms beside the meadows of the River Axe.

Historical interest: Sadborow House; Forde Abbey.

Natural history: Buzzards, duck and heron.

THIS REWARDING seven mile walk explores the countryside around Thorncombe in the far west of Dorset, passing Forde Abbey and the classical lines of Sadborow House. If you are planing to combine the walk with a visit to Forde Abbey itself, G. D. Roper opens parts of his house and its thirty acre grounds for the National Gardens Scheme on Easter Sunday and Monday, and on each Wednesday, Sunday and bank holiday between May to September. The opening hours are from 2.00 pm to 6.00 pm and teas are available. The other appeal for walkers is that this is varied countryside, always interesting and changing, without any steep climbs and with paths that are easy to find. What does need stressing, however, is that after the winter rains much of this Axe valley countryside is perpetually damp and rubber boots are essential if you are doing this walk at any time except during a drought. **Approach Thorncombe from the B 3165, the road from Lyme Regis to Crewkerne. You turn west from it at the Rose and Crown, Birdsmoorgate, which is eight miles from Lyme.** Continue along this lane for nearly two miles (ignoring a turning at Sadborow) to a crossroads with a tiny stone-roofed cottage. Turn right here and drive into Thorncombe village. Park in the centre of Thorncombe, in the main street near its junction with Chard Street. The road is wide enough here for parking.

The walk begins at this corner beside the Gospel Hall. To its left a track runs beside a barn into a small farmyard. Go straight ahead after the first iron gate, through a second gate into the field facing you. A public footpath runs along the side

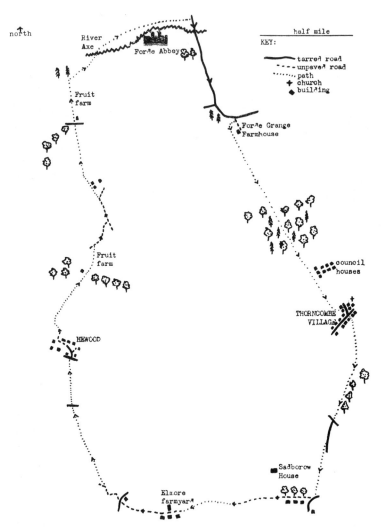

north

River
Axe

Forde Abbey

Fruit
farm

Forde Grange
Farmhouse

Fruit
farm

council
houses

HEWOOD

THORNCOMBE
VILLAGE

Sadborow
House

Elmore
farmyard

of the hill to the end of the field. Here there is an iron gate and you continue straight ahead, keeping to the top of the field by the trees. **Look out for a spot where you can cross from this field into the higher field to the right, above the trees.** In this next field the path follows the top edge of the valley, which becomes increasingly deep-cut and wooded. **At the end of this field there is a**

stile and you now walk just inside the edge of the wood. A couple of well-made bridges carry the path along the top of the ravine. The path then follows and crosses the stream, bringing you to a stile and a large field.

Turn right at this point, and walk towards the house and road sign. Cross the road, following the second road that runs straight ahead, signposted to Sadborow.

Hewood and the track down to the wood.

After about 200 yards there is a small wooden gate in the bank on the right-hand side of the road. Go through this and turn sharply left, as the public path follows the left-hand hedgerow, parallel with the road. On the other side of the field is Sadborow House, a three storey Hamstone mansion, built between 1773 and 1775 bp John Bragge at a cost of £2,589 2s. 4½d. The account book of its daily work and expenses is preserved in the Dorset County Museum.

At the end of the field is a wooden gate in the corner and you walk on to a bend in the road. But don't follow the tarred road. Almost immediately there is a gap in the wall on the right-hand side and a farm track leads to some barns. There are tall beech trees beside this bridleway, which then runs between the fields, with Sadborow to your right. The dirt track then swings to the left but you continue straight ahead, passing a cattle trough, to the wooden gate in the hedgerow facing you. Its gateposts belong to another age, that of Mr Bragge's ex-pense book.

The track is then a well defined green lane, bringing you in half a mile to a dirt track through Elmore farmyard and on to the tarred road. Its ancient buildings are mostly heaps of rubble.

Cross the tarred road, by the bungalow, on to another dirt track. You follow it around two bends and then keep on it when the main farm track branches off into a field. The older path continues through a wooden gate and is a narrow old cartway with a gravel base and a high fern-covered banks on each side. It brings you to a field. Follow the left-hand hedgerow to the tarred road. Cross the road, and continue through the right-hand of the two gates facing you, the wooden one. Follow the left-hand hedgerow, and likewise in the next field. You come to another road.

Cross the road and follow the lane on the other side to "Hewood only". 'Huewood' is how it is pronounced, or 'Yarward' if you happen to live there. They still talk about one of its best known characters, the keeper Jim Guppy. This hamlet has a dozen buildings, half of them still thatched, set attractively around the four sides of what was its common — and still grass covered and with geese and peacock. It is the nearest there is to an unspoilt rural community in these parts, not the least of its charms being that it still has agricultural cottagers.

From the far corner of the green, a track passes an 'L' shaped range of thatched cottages and leads into a field of grass and bullrushes that slopes down towards the woods in the distance. Follow the track across the top part of the field, through a gate into a second field. In this field you follow the right-hand hedgerow. This brings you to a second gate and a stony hedged trackway that crosses the stream.

On the other side you pass a cottage, walk along the right-hand side of its lawn. This is East Cottage, and the nearest a car can get to it is a field away. After you have crossed this field, the path then passes through six acres or raspberries and loganberries.

After the raspberries you turn right along a hedged track and climb to the top of the slope. Follow the main track to the left at the top, for about a hundred yards, and then continue straight ahead, across some generally muddy ground, keeping the buildings to your right.

After the farmyard you follow the right-hand side of the next field, through a wooden gate, and then downhill to the right-hand end of the wood facing you. Cross the tarred road. A signpost points to "Forde Bridge" and you walk through another fruit farm. At the end of the raspberries you walk into the larch trees and turn immediately right. There is a stile into the field, which has the outlines of some mediaeval houses.

A bridge takes you over a stream, by a waterfall, and then you come to a concrete footbridge over the River Axe. On the other side you turn right, into the meadow, and follow the river upstream, with Forde Abbey across the water to your right. The railway line is to your left.

In half a mile you come to a tarred road and turn right, in the direction of Forde Abbey. Pass the Abbey gates and walk uphill, continuing straight ahead at the road junction. In about 200 yards, just around the bend, you turn right at the entrance to Forde Grange Farm, and then immediately right again — through a wooden gate. Turn left in this field, keeping the farmhouse and its garden to your left on the other side of the hedge. At the end of the field you take the right-hand of the two gates facing you, and walk uphill keeping the hedge to your left. Near the top you cross a field.

Towards the right-hand side of the wood facing you there is a gap in the hedge. Walk straight through the wood to the other side. Much of the ground has been dug out for gravel and stone. Keep walking straight ahead so that you come out on the south side. Here there is a council estate visible on the left part of the skyline in front of you. But if you see it to your right, you are too low down the wood and will have to walk back up the hill.

Midway along the south side of the wood there is a gate into the field and you then follow the hedge, passing to the right of the housing estate. From now on the older section of Thorncombe is clearly visible, and you aim for a point to the right of the church tower. An alleyway brings you into a side street. Turn right and walk back to your car. □

Lambert's Castle and Charmouth Forest

Distance: 5 miles.
Difficult bits: Nothing of consequence.
State of paths: Reasonable to good.
Scenery: The edge of the far west Dorset hills, heavily wooded towards Charmouth and Monkton Wyld.
Historical interest: Lambert's Castle Hill (National Trust) with its hill-fort, site of semaphore station and racecourse.
Natural history: Horse-tails and marsh flowers; hedgerows thick with mountain ash; buzzards overhead.

A TRIVIAL boundary change took place twenty years ago to enable Dorset and Devon to split some roadmaking on equal terms. There were no residents to be affected, but the result was that the 839-ft plateau of Lambert's Castle Hill was transferred from Devon into Dorset. This was very much Dorset's gain as the great hilltop is National Trust property — on the B 3165 between Lyme Regis and Crewkerne — with superb views and a varied ecology. This *five* mile walk through the small woods of the Dorset-Devon border is based on Lambert's Castle, but make sure that you do not miss the castle itself. There is a small National Trust car park on the hilltop, but our parking instructions are different, because the Trust's compound is unsigned and very difficult to locate unless you are already familiar with the hill. The main road, at the top of this slope, is not the place for much hesitation, and the county council has already blocked off one access point.

However, you can walk to the official car park; its location is described at the end of the article. On finding the car park you can firstly put 25p in the slot to pay for your own parking, and then look at the notice board showing the Napoleonic war semaphore station (see next page), and the layout of the Iron Age hillfort at the north end of the spur. The area between the notice board and the fort was laid out as a racecourse in the 19th century. From the double banks of the fort, on a clear day, you can look across the Marshwood Vale to Portland. The signal station seems to have been in the north-east part of the hill-fort, beyond a small prehistoric burial mound, and its signals were from Toller Down to Stockland Hill. The latter, in the west, is easier to spot as it now has a high, white, television mast. On the western slopes of the hill

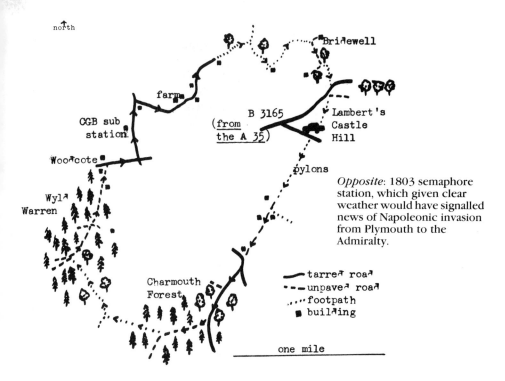

north

Bridewell

farm

CGB sub
station

B 3165
(from
the A 35)

Lambert's
Castle
Hill

Woodcote

pylons

Wyld
Warren

Opposite: 1803 semaphore
station, which given clear
weather would have signalled
news of Napoleonic invasion
from Plymouth to the
Admiralty.

Charmouth
Forest

———— tarred road
– – –unpaved road
....footpath
▪ building

one mile

there is a hanging beech wood.

Recently the National Trust has
laid some wire across parts of the fort
banks, to reduce soil erosion, and this
is not the only threat it faces. The
interior, on the day we researched the
walk, had the unmistakeable signs of
fresh metal detector activity. As one
would normally expect few metal
finds from this kind of site, it may be
an indication that the flat-topped hill
was reused as a Roman shrine, or the
material may have been from its later
sheep-fair days. There are several
trenches and a raised platform on this
part of the hill.

**Lambert's Castle Hill is on the B3165,
nine miles south-west of Crewkerne.** If
you come from the east, along the A
35, keep on the main road for three
miles after Charmouth (ignoring the
turn-off to Lyme Regis)and take the
turning on the right signposted to

Crewkerne. Lambert's Castle is in
four miles.

**On the top of Lambert's Castle Hill,
between the beech wood and the tall
power lines that cross the main road,
there is a signpost pointing you east to
"Fishpond".** Take this lane and park
on the left, about 200 yards from the
corner, where there is an opening and
a gravel track. Although there are no
signs, this is National Trust land.

**After you have left your car you
continue along the tarred road, away
from the main road, for about fifty
yards. Then turn right down an old
trackway.** It has a firm base of large
pebbles, and runs between high
hedgerows. This ancient road passes
beneath a 160 feet high pylon, not an
unimpressive sight. You reach some
buildings and the track continues
straight ahead, downhill, beneath
some large beech trees. At the foot of

16

the hill you come to a tarred road. Continue straight ahead, along the right hand fork — signposted to Wootton Fitzpaine. This road passes through a beechwood and at the corner facing you, where the road climbs uphill, there is a sign: "Forestry Commission, Charmouth".

Leave the road at this point, and continue straight ahead along the gravel track. Continue along it for about 200 yards, to another sign, and fork right along a narrower, older, trackway. This brings you out of the trees, into open countryside, and you walk down to a clearing, where the main track bends sharply left.

Here you take the grassy path that leads to the right, and then to the left, to a field gate that looks across a small valley to woodland on the other side. Walk down this slope to the stream, near the bottom right-hand corner of the field. The stream is forded at this point and you can step across the stones.

Continue straight ahead up the slope facing you, to a wooden gate into the wood. Go straight across the woodland ride, heading uphill between some birch trees. The track then climbs beside a bank, on the other side of which is a field. At the end of this section the track bends to the left and then continues uphill into

17

a denser area of wood. At the top of the hill there is a wide track.

Turn right along this forest road. You come to a crossroads (beside a television aerial) and keep straight ahead, continuing uphill. This brings you in half a mile to the tarred road, at Woodcote Farm.

Turn right, and walk a third of a mile to the crossroads. Turn left here, along the road sign posted to "Hawkchurch". After the entrance to the Woodvale electricity substation you come in a hundred yards to a cottage and a turning on the right, with a sign to "Lower Stonebarrow".

Walk along this road. In half a mile, the track passes a farmyard. Finally, at the end of the made-up section, in another third of a mile, you pass a cottage and walk downhill through a holly wood (ignoring another footpath that branches off to the left).

Towards the foot of the hill there are two small fields to your right, and you go through a wooden gate into the second of them. Walk straight ahead towards the far left hand end of the field, but cross into the next field, to the left, at a dip crossed by a small stream.

On the other side you turn right, and walk through a gap in the hedgerow facing you. At the top of this field there is a cottage and a disused farmyard.

Turn left at this point, keeping the upper hedgerow of this field immediately on your right. At the end of the field you slip under the wire on to an attractive length of unspoilt green lane. This climbs uphill, and becomes a gravel track, after you pass the entrance to Bridewell. You are now climbing the foothills of Lambert's Castle. There is a straight stretch of track, with open ground to your right, and at the top of this slope the main path bends to the right, between some holly bushes.

Here you turn left, through a wooden gate. Then turn immediately right, to follow the hedgerow uphill This hedge is laden with mountain ash berries in the second half of the year. At the top you slip under the wire and climb on to the road.

Turn right, taking care to be seen by the traffic. Leave the road at the top of the rise. There is a National Trust sign, and this is Lambert's Castle Hill. Strike off across the peaty heathland — a flat expanse of purple moor grass — aiming for a point midway between the first and second pylons from the left. But if you wish to explore the hilltop first, continue straight ahead along the rough track. ☐

18

Pilsdon Pen
and Lewesdon Hill

Distance: 6 miles.
Difficult bits: Energetic climbs.
State of paths: Some undergrowth in high summer and mud in winter.
Scenery: Outstanding, including the highest hill Dorset at the edge of the Marshwood Vale; deep-cut valleys.
Historical interest: Pilsdon Pen hill-fort (National Trust); much smaller fortifications on Lewesdon Hill (also National Trust); Burstock Grange; Broadwindsor Toll House; 'Charles II slept here' (in Broadwindsor).
Natural history: Buzzard, badger, fox and roe-deer country.
Literary associations: William Crowe's poem about Lewesdon Hill.

AUTUMN CONDITIONS encourage an expedition to the ramparts of the Marshwood Vale. Dorset's most demanding walking country has two main twin peaks which are the objectives scaled in this *six mile walk*. "As much akin as Leuson hill to Pilsen-pen," is the way a west Dorset expression was first recorded, in 1662. "Completely unlike" is what it means. For Pilsdon Pen is a western moor, rising like a treeless tor of decaying granite, bristling with whortleberries amongst rough tufts of matted grass. Its hard embattled lines belong to the West. Lewesdon's character is a total contrast and belongs to the East. These softer curves inspired a lengthy romantic verse from the 18th cen-

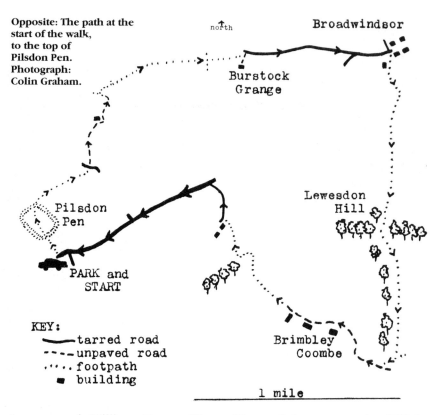

Opposite: The path at the start of the walk, to the top of Pilsdon Pen. Photograph: Colin Graham.

north

Broadwindsor

Burstock Grange

Lewesdon Hill

Pilsdon Pen

PARK and START

KEY:
——— tarred road
- - - - unpaved road
· · · · · footpath
▪ building

Brimbley Coombe

1 mile

tury pen of William Crowe. The hanging beech woods of Lewesdon feel out of place on Devonian rocks and copy the atmosphere of famous chalkland beauty spots in Kent and Surrey. Both Dorset summits share the same foothills, sliced by deep-cut gorges that spawn more than twenty streams. Those that make for Lyme Bay become the lifeforce of the green dairy pastures of the enchanted Marshwood Vale. Drivers coming westward for this walk should head for Maiden Newton, Beaminster and Broadwindsor. The B3164 runs from Broadwindsor to Birdsmoorgate. Halfway between these two places, two miles out from Broadwindsor and at the foot of the highest hill in sight, is a layby for

15 cars. It is next to a sign "Pilsdon 1" and you park at the roadside viewpoint.

Park and start in this layby. Cross the road to a gate in the hedgerow. Open this and climb straight to the top. At 908 feet it is the highest point in Dorset and, naturally, is crowned by solid Iron Age fortifications.

Archaeology of this major National Trust hill-fort: *Three banks with ditches between them, built by iron-using Celtic settlers from across the Channel after 200 BC. These enclose about nine acres of a flat-topped spur. They were defended by slings, firing rounded pebbles. Excavation has revealed areas of stained soil that mark the*

20

sites of wattle and daub huts and a spread of coarse blackened pottery. Gold-making crucibles were the outstanding finds, together with what appears to be the only pre-Roman Celtic temple in Dorset. It was a large building, about 50 yards square, and would have been considered Roman but for the discovery of hoards of slingstone along its foundations. The dig, which took place from 1963-71, also uncovered evidence that Pilsdon Pen may have been one of the native fortresses stormed by Vespasian's Second Legion, about AD 45-46.

Walk ahead across the centre of the fort, over the traces of excavations, to the far right-hand corner of the defences. A path passes through a gap in the gorse and the ramparts. Hawthorn trees grow on an old bank that marks the divide between farmland and prehistory. Descend from the hilltop.

Follow the left-hand side of the hawthorn downhill. Climb a stile and then go through a gate to come out at a bend in a tarred lane.

Cross straight over and continue down a stony track. Turn right at the farm buildings and walk beside three asbestos barns. Follow the

Lewesdon's beech wood. Photograph: Colin Graham.

track beside the right-hand hedge and keep on this when it forks right through a black metal gate.

Next there is a concrete bridge beside a water trough. Fork right immediately after you cross the bridge. Facing you, but rather obscured in the centre of the hedge, there is a wooden gate.

Walk up to this and cross into the next field. Continue diagonally to the first gate on the right-hand side. Go through this and follow the left hedgerow. Continue straight ahead at the end of this field. Walk ahead through the gate facing you and ignore the other track which you cross. At Burstock Grange you come out on to the drive of the house which in a few yards joins a tarred road.

Turn right and walk into Broadwindsor. When you enter the village, just after the "30 limit" sign, there is a cottage on the right called "The Toll House". Beside it is a track signposted "Footpath, Lewesdon

Hill ¾".

Walk this, across a stream and a stile, and then diagonally over to the top corner of the first field. Here, under the maple tree on the other side of the fence, a badger lay dead outside its sett on the day when we researched this walk.

Continue ahead along the top of the ridge that follows the streambed. Walk through the gateway facing you, and keep straight on to the next. Walk up the hillside to a similar gap in the next hedgerow and continue ahead beside the beech trees until there is a stile and you enter the woods.

Keep walking uphill to the 893-foot top of this National Trust property. There is a Trust signpost at the bottom and another at the top. Continue walking up the slope, in a leftish direction, until you come to this second sign on the eastern peak of Lewesdon Hill.

Keep straight on and descend. At the foot of the bracken-covered slope there is a line of beech trees on an old boundary. Veer left through these trees and follow the path left again when a fallen trunk lies in the way. You find yourself in a belt of scrubland that runs outwards as a spur from the main woods on the hill. On the left there is a field and you can look across to the masts of the Rampisham radio station. As a general guide, if you become mystified by the multitude of paths, you should be walking due south. **The path emerges on a dirt track. Turn right and this then joins another, more stony, farm road. Turn right along it to Brimbley Coombe Farm.** The main track forks right to Lower Brimbley Coombe. Here you go through the black gate beside the right-hand wall of the yellow stone building at the head of the valley.

Follow this deep-cut track into a field. Walk beside the right-hand hedgerow. Carry on through a black metal gate and continue to follow the farm track beside the hedge. It passes through a second black gate and curves left around a wooded gully. Another black gate stands at the top of the next rise. Do not open this but follow the main track uphill to the right, round the bend. At the top, follow the left-hand hedgerow and keep walking ahead until you have passed close to two houses and come to a black metal gate opening on to a partly-tarred track. Grass grows in the middle of this road.

Turn right along this drive and continue to the junction with the tarred road. Here you turn left and walk back to your car which is a mile away. ☐

'King Charles II slept here September 23-24, 1651' on his flight from the Battle of Worcester – not that he would recognise this Broadwindsor cottage as it was burnt to the ground and rebuilt in 1902. Photograph: Frederick G. Masters.

Stonebarrow Hill and the River Char

> IMPORTANT CHANGES: When the Charmouth Bypass has been completed, through the middle of this walk, it will be the A35 and you will have to turn off for Newlands House and Stonebarrow Lane. You'll also find it cuts across the meadows between the Toll House and Befferlands Farm. You still take the lane towards Catherston Leweston but follow it a little further, over the bridge across the bypass, and then immediately turn right along the footpath that follows the fence of the bypass until you reach the River Char. Then resume your course upstream.

Distance: 6 miles.

Difficult bits: None.

State of paths: Damp in the vale except in high summer; hill-paths well marked.

Scenery: Pastoral – two miles of river bank through the Marshwood Vale, with the wild bulk of the National Trust's Stonebarrow Hill and coastal landslips offering a complete contrast.

Historical interest: Charmouth toll-house.

Natural history: Swans at Charmouth; wild flowers in the unimproved meadows.

THE NATIONAL Trust is the largest landowner on the six miles of scenic coast between Charmouth and Eype. Its ownership is far more extensive than it appears on the ground, for as well as the clifftops the Trust rents many hundreds of acres between the sea and the A 35 trunk road to tenant farmers. The result is some of the best public access possibilities that Dorset can offer.

Drive on to Stonebarrow Hill from the A 35 at Charmouth. Turn off the main A 35 at the east end of Charmouth village at the foot of a steep hill. There is a caravan site close by and the turning is signposted "Stonebarrow Lane". However, what you are more likely to spot is a large black and white board saying "Newlands House". Take the road beside this board — it has a "no through road" sign — and climb the hill. Drive to the top.

Cross a cattle-grid and then pass a "No unauthorised camping" sign. After this sign there is a wide grass clearing, which is a National Trust picnic area, and you park your car here. This is Stonebarrow Hill and most of the land it overlooks is part of the Trust's Golden Cap estate.

Walk back to the "No unauthorised camping" sign and turn to your left along a stony track. After about 30 paces you pass a gate on your right, and then after a further 20 paces there is a gap in the hedgerow and you turn right through this. Follow the right-hand fence to a sign on the horizon which says "Cain's Folly". The folly was to build on these slipping cliffs, and even the 1940 invasion defences have been carried towards the sea by post-war landslides.

Turn right at this sign, across a stile, and walk along the cliff path

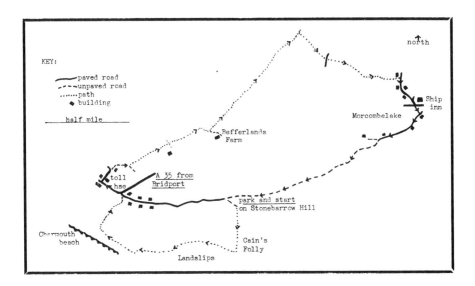

KEY:

KEY:
- paved road
- unpaved road
- path
- building

half mile

toll
hse

A 35 from
Bridport

Befferlands
Farm

Morcombelake

Ship
inn

north

park and start
on Stonebarrow Hill

Charmouth
beach

Cain's
Folly

Landslips

towards **Charmouth.** Lyme Regis and its Cobb harbour are in the second bay. The path runs downhill for a mile to the footbridge below Charmouth beach.

Do not cross the bridge but turn to the right, cross a stile, and follow the river bank. This is the Char. A pair of swans nest in spring upstream from the bridge. The path along the bank is clear, and at the end of the field it enters a patch of scrub. The public path now looks down on the water and skirts a wooded garden before joining a dirt track which comes out on the main road.

Turn left, cross the bridge, and keep to the footpath on the left-hand side of the road. On the opposite side, you pass a brick-built turnpike company toll house which has wide overhanging eaves.

Twenty paces after the toll house you cross the road and turn right, along the road signposted to "Catherston Leweston and Wootton Fitzpaine". Walk along this road just over a hundred yards to the corner.

Continue straight ahead at this corner, over a cattle-grid, on to a rough track beside a concrete block-wall. Some fifty yards after the end of this farmyard wall the track (which runs past caravans) bends to the right, to a sewage works.

At this bend there is a gate beside an electricity pole. Go through this gate and walk along the well-marked track across two fields. In the following field there is no visible path but the right-of-way is now easy to find as it follows the nearside bank of the River Char. At the end of this field you go through the gate, and walk straight across the next field to the right-hand of the two gates facing you. Follow the left-hand hedgerow. At the end of this field there is a gate and you are now back on the river bank, though it has now diminished to almost stream-size, and on the opposite side there is a caravan camp.

At the end of the field after the caravans you cross an ancient but abandoned trackway, which led from

25

Stanton St Gabriel on the coast inland to Wootton Fitzpaine. It is now a rather pretty ditch. Follow the "Whitchurch" pointer into the next field. Where they do not plant caravans, the fields of this valley are lush pastures and you are now at the seaward end of the Marshwood Vale, which is still Dorset's best dairying country.

Summertime visitors to Charmouth swan about by the river.

As a farmhouse comes into view, on the other side of the river, you will see a bridge across the river. The path is now on the other side of the

Friesian dip: this is still dairy country.

water. To the right of the path, the field has the banks and ditches of what appears to be an otherwise destroyed mediaeval mill and leet. **Do not go up the slope into the yard of Befferlands Farm but continue following the stream.** Cross the fence, and over two railway sleepers into the first field, and gradually cross to the higher side of the field. The path now follows the right-hand hedgerow but is still within sight of the stream. By the end of the field you are again above the water, and in the next field you follow the left-hand hedgerow for about 40 paces to a dirt track which descends the bank to a footbridge across a deep ditch.

Cross the footbridge and on the other side turn right, and then left to follow the main stream. You are now in a long, narrow meadow which is beside the stream.

At the far end of the meadow there is another footbridge, also with a white-painted rail. You cross this but then turn abruptly right and follow the right-hand hedgerow, beside a small brook. You are now walking towards the gap between Hardown Hill (left) and Chardown and Stonebarrow. At the end of this field, near the right-hand corner, there are fence-bars on to the tarred road. Here, whilst researching the walk, we met a young farmer and his wife who stopped from their work to explain the course of the path towards Hardown Hill. They went on to say how beautiful the stream path was through the Marshwood Vale, and said it would be a good thing when the route was properly waymarked. They did not begrudge having to provide stiles for walkers. Countryside walking becomes a complete pleasure when one is made to feel welcome.

Cross straight over the tarred road and into the field opposite. Follow the left-hand hedgerow. Go over the fence in the top left-hand corner of the field and continue straight ahead to the far left-hand corner of the next field. Go through this fence and continue ahead, aiming for the gate in the hedge which faces you. Then continue ahead to the power line on the other side of the field, into a corner of the field near some trees. Here, beside a hawthorn, there is a gap in the hedge as you look in the direction of the houses on the side of Hardown Hill.

Go through this gap and walk uphill towards the buildings on Hardown Hill, following the right-hand hedgerow. There is a gap at the top right-hand end of the field and you go through this into the next field. Follow the left-hand hedgerow uphill to the top left-hand corner of this field. Here there is a gate on to the tarred road.

Turn right, and walk towards Morcombelake. Go down to the main road and cross over, to a narrow lane on the other side from the Ship Inn. This lane only runs for about 50 yards and you then turn right, heading uphill along a "no through road". The tarred part of this road ends at Greenlands Farm and you then walk uphill through an iron gate and up a flinty track to the top of Stonebarrow Hill. The track looks across the Marshwood Vale to a familiar west Dorset skyline — the triple heights (from right to left) of Lewesdon, Pilsdon Pen and Lambert's Castle. **On top of the hill you go through a gate, pass a National Trust "No camping" sign, and then continue straight ahead along the main track and back to your car, which is about half-a-mile away.** □

The Walk to Golden Cap

Distance: 7 miles.
Difficult bits: Some hill-climbs.
State of paths: Good; generally well-marked though with some misleading notices and awkward stiles.
Scenery: Superb; unspoilt meadows and wild cliffs, including Golden Cap – the highest point on the south coast (618 feet). All of it is National Trust land. Fine views from Portland to Start Point.
Historical interest: St Gabriel's church (from a distance); cairns on Golden Cap; plaque to the Earl of Antrim.
Natural history: Buzzards, roe-deer and wild flowers.

WHEN YOU hear that some medi-aeval pile is the jewel in the National Trust crown, think instead of Golden Cap cliff on the seaboard of west Dorset. Here the National Trust has achieved conservation of the scenery on a scale that has saved an entire landscape. This *seven* mile walk begins above Char-mouth at Westhay Farm which was given to the Trust in 1961. Six other farms, providing six miles of rugged cliff between Charmouth and West Bay, were bought by the Trust's Enterprise Neptune campaign in the mid-1960s.

Since then the western and inland sides of the estate have been stretched into a holding that totals 1,914½ acres — only five and a half short of being precisely three square miles. It is an achievement for which the Trust nationally and particularly at their understaffed Wessex regional office beside Stourhead gardens can be totally proud, for it is a famous victory salvaged from the two decades in which intensive farming changed the face of lowland England. The

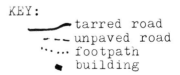

KEY:

⎯⎯⎯ tarred road
- - - unpaved road
······ footpath
• building

Golden Cap estate is a landscape of the past. In the past fifteen years little or no hedgecutting has been done in many of the valleys, and all the hedgerows of the small fields have been preserved. The damp conditions and mild maritime climate have led to a jungle growth of the hedge vegetation into great clumps as high as a house. There is nowhere else in Dorset where you can experience traditional — neglected, say farming cynics — pastureland on this scale, extending as far as you can see.

Walking conditions are generally delightful, though here and there it is inevitable that you cross the spring-line and there is a shortage of footpath markers. If you keep reading the magazine you will stay on the right course of path, but the public path is often the lesser of two options and in the absence of a sign it is easy to make a slip. In other places there are notices asking you not to stray from the path but nothing to tell you where the path is — a far more useful application of signing would be direc-tion arrows for the line of the right-of-way. Much random walking was taking place as a result of the confusion on the day that we researched the walk. The other problem was a frequent use of fence-bars instead of stiles. These bars are unusually high and older people were finding them a struggle. Because of the small size of the average pasture the next tended to be only 50 feet away and the walk became an obstacle course. A little effort is a low price to pay for the outstanding scenery that is on offer, but the public notices small irritations.

This walk also shows what has happened to the non-National Trust coast lands. If you pause at the seat in the pine wood on Langdon Hill you will be looking beyond the Trust's hedges to the ploughed fields and caravans instead of furze bushes and meadows. It could all so easily have gone the way of everywhere else.

Drive on to Stonebarrow Hill from the A35 at the east end of Charmouth village. There, at the foot of

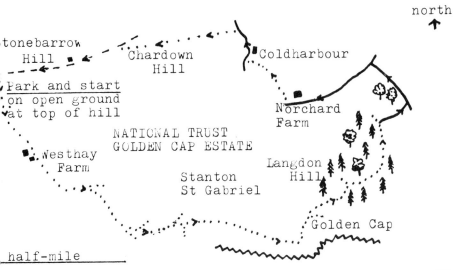

north

tonebarrow Hill

Chardown Hill

Coldharbour

Park and start on open ground at top of hill

Norchard Farm

NATIONAL TRUST GOLDEN CAP ESTATE

Westhay Farm

Langdon Hill

Stanton St Gabriel

Golden Cap

half-mile

29

the steep hill that drops down from the Bridport direction, is a caravan site and a turning on the south side of road signposted "Stonebarrow Lane". There is a large notice board for "Newlands Hotel". Take the road beside this board. It has a no through road sign. Climb the hill. It is a narrow lane though it was once the main coach road from Exeter to Dorchester. Drive with extreme caution and sound your horn at corners as these days it carries an excessive number of cars. Also beware of walkers trapped between the cars and obscured banks. Drive to the top and cross the cattle-grid into the National Trust picnic area.

After the National Trust's "You are now on the Golden Cap Estate" sign there is ample parking on the grassy top of Stonebarrow Hill. Beside the Trust's sign there is a bridleway pointer, arrowed towards

Golden Cap from Westhay and (opposite) from the only higher thing around – the sky. National Trust photographs.

the sea. Follow the line of this pointer, through a gap in the car park fence, keeping on the left of an attractively windswept length of old hedgerow. In 150 yards you cross another bridleway and continue straight ahead downhill, through the gorse thickets, heading towards Westhay Farm which is in the valley about 200 yards from the sea.

At the end of the gorse you pass a footpath notice board and continue straight ahead downhill along a concrete farm road. The notice on the gate reads: "Public Footpath. No Horses".

After Westhay Farm the track bends to the left, and then disappears in a field. Here you walk across the lower part of the field to

the gap in the hedge in the opposite corner. Cross Westhay Water, a shallow stream, and continue straight ahead uphill. At the end of the field there is an iron gate but you go across the fence posts instead, about 40 feet to the right of it. Follow the left-hand hedgerow down to the Ridge Water stream. On the other side the path forks left and then right, uphill, and you keep the hedgerow to your right. Half way up the hill you go through a gap in the hedgerow, pass a ruined barn, and walk up to the gate on the skyline.

From here you are aiming towards the wooded hill-line left of Golden Cap and skirt an expanding landslip. Climb the fence posts on the other side and follow the edge of the slippage, and then go across it — with care if there has been more ground falling away since this was

written in 1983 — towards the right-hand end of Golden Cap. Near the corner of the next field there is another set of fence posts for you to clamber over. Turn right on the other side, to a further set in 50 yards. Keep towards the edge of the cliff. At the bottom of the field there is a footpath sign pointing to: "Golden Cap ¾, Seatown 1½".

The path goes down to a footbridge and you then climb to the top of Golden Cap. On the left, three fields away, is the ruin of St Gabriel's church, abandoned when the village of Morcombelake, in the distance, sprang up on the slopes of Hardown Hill. The settlement of Stanton around the old church is completely sheltered from the winds. There were 23 families living here, in cottages around the green, in 1650. It was in 1824 that the old road across Stonebarrow Hill, the one you drove up from Charmouth

31

and which now forms the National Trust's linear car-parking area, was replaced by the present line of the A35 through Morcombelake. By then the church at Stanton was a derelict hiding place for smugglers' kegs.

Continue to the top of Golden Cap. At the top there are a couple of ancient cairns, four feet high, and a block of Portland stone with an ammonite crest and slate plaque: "Golden Cap. Given by members of the National Trust and friends in memory of the Earl of Antrim KBE, Chairman of the National Trust from 1966 until his death in 1977." The actual top of the hill, though it had been used as the estate's name for a decade before, only came into the Trust's ownership in 1978. It was bought as Antrim's memorial and it has the distinction, at 618 feet, of being the highest cliff on the south coast. The view down to the waters and Seatown Beach is stupendous, with Start Point to Portland in the distance on a clear day.

From the memorial stone the track leads to an Ordnance Survey pillar. Turn left here, downhill in a northward direction aiming for the centre of the pine plantation. You come to a three-way footpath signpost. Continue straight ahead, towards "Langdon Hill, Chideock". Cross the fence into the next field and follow the hedgerow to the other side. Here you go through the gate and turn left into the wood, which has a National Trust notice reminding you not to drop matches or cigarette ends. The wood has an unusual mix of Scots pine with an undergrowth of holly. **Half way up the slope you come to a ride and turn right** along it. This skirts around the east side of the hill, beside younger beech trees

overlooking Seatown and Chideock. A viewpoint has been cleared and a seat provided. Continue along the ride to the car park.

Here you turn right, downhill. Follow the gravel road to the left at the National Trust and "Forestry Commission Chideock" signs.

Turn left at the tarred road, passing the notice "No Parking beyond this point". Follow the road to Norchard Farm, in half a mile.

Turn right immediately after the barn, through the gate into the field. Follow the hedgerow uphill to the damp area at the corner and cross the fence posts. Continue straight ahead uphill, a little leftward of the bungalow, Cold Harbour, to the fence posts on to a gravel track. Turn right along it, passing the bungalow. Cold Harbour as a name — cold arbour, implying a hut where travellers stopped for the night — has been linked with Saxon usage of the Roman road system, and this may be an indication that the road from Exeter to Dorchester passed over Stonebarrow Hill.

In about 300 yards you come to a wooden gate and just before it some fence posts, on the left. Cross these and follow the hedgerow uphill. At the top you go through a five-barred gate and continue straight ahead on the other side towards Lyme Regis. Follow the scrubby hedgerow at the top of the hill to a gate and collection of signs.

Go through the gate into the car-park and walk along the gravel road, still keeping the scrubby hedgerow to your right. Your car is in about half-a-mile, after the National Trust information office, an ex-Ministry of Defence coastal radar building, which explains the ten feet high security fencing. □

Golden Cap and Thorncombe Beacon

Distance: 7 miles.
Difficult bits: A couple of stiff climbs.
State of paths: Good, apart from a watery lane.
Scenery: Magnificent National Trust cliffs – Thorncombe Beacon at 507 feet and Golden Cap at 618 – and deep-cut lanes.
Historical interest: Cairns on Golden Cap; St Gabriel's church; traditional farmyard at Shedbush Bottom.
Natural history: Buzzards, roe deer, rabbits, wild flowers; "Remember to feed the badger" – instruction given to National Trust holiday cottagers at Stanton St Gabriel; interesting breeds of sheep at Silverbridge Farm.

DORSET'S MOST rugged and wild coastline runs between Bridport and Charmouth where extensive areas of land are in the hands of the National Trust. This *seven* mile walk is especially tough because of steep climbs but all the paths are easy to follow. Don't be tempted to start the walk if the higher cliffs are shrouded in fog; the cloud level may lower and in places there is not even a barbed wire fence to stop you stumbling over the cliff. Otherwise this walk only demands energy and will give you all the grandeur of west Dorset and its constantly changing landscape. The hill country that conceals the A 35 road westward of Bridport is some of the most beautiful and unspoilt in Dorset.

Turn south from the A 35 at Chideock, turning off the main street in the middle of the village — into Seahill Lane which is signposted to "Seatown". In a mile you come to the sea and park on the left, opposite the Anchor Inn (Ordnance Survey map reference SY 420 917). Start off in this direction, passing to the seaward side of the inn. Spot the big anchor lying outside, which was re-covered in 1986 from the 1749 wreck of the treasure-ship *Hope*, from Amsterdam, lying off the Chesil Beach. The cliff path starts beside the public lavatories. Head for a National Trust sign above the undercliff and continue to the left of it.

Follow the footpath to the top of Golden Cap. Shun the easier options that are signed inland! The last part of the climb is very steep and when you reach the top you will be standing on the highest cliff of the English South Coast, at an altitude of 618 feet above the adjacent sea-level.

Pass the memorial to National Trust chairman the Earl of Antrim. Make sure you admire the ammonite cast in the back of his Purbeck boulder. It was in his memory that the headland was bought, for the nation, after his death in 1977.

Hereon the only way is down, in the direction of "Charmouth 3" and Lyme Regis. On entering the first field you turn right and then head left of centre, inland to the bottom corner of the field and the greystone ruin of St Gabriel's church. This is the remains of a 14th century building which ended useful life as a smugglers' hiding place.

Turn left and then pass the surviving buildings of St Gabriel's village. Follow the concreted road that leads away from the house. You are now heading inland, up the valley, and the next building you pass is Norchard House.

Turn left through the second gate after the farm. Follow this path across a field to a thatched cottage. The path turns sharply to the left and you pass Shedbush Bottom farmyard which dates from about 1700. Having gone through a gate you are on a track which brings you into the village of Morcombelake.

Turn right on to the main road. Take the first road left, up Sun Lane. Turn left at the end of this lane and then go right, through the gate beneath an oak tree halfway up the hill. Cross this field in a leftward direction to the opposite corner, at the end of a plantation. Pass over a stream.

Bear right around the plantation and walk diagonally up the field to the gate. Turn right. Go straight across the next field which brings you into Silverbridge Farm. This farm has flocks of Clun Forest and Jacob sheep.

Note: Most of this footpath you have just walked from Morcombelake is not public but we have the kind permission of Major Weld of Chideock Manor to use it. A public path does run across these fields but at the time of writing it was difficult to find. It may, however, be reinstated in the future, or diverted on to the alternative route.

Turn left on the road at Silverbridge Farm where a signpost points to "North Chideock only".

Turn right at the junction in North Chideock and fork right at the house where an old fir tree stands on a triangle of grass in the middle of the road. This tarred road becomes a track after Hell Farm. For a short way the road has been taken over by a stream. A local farmer suggests that any of you who get wet feet should write to Dorset County Council and ask for a nine inch pipe to be put under the road. It is the council's road and it climbs Quarr Hill, a favourite haunt of the buzzard. At the top the old road passes through a cool hollow overhung by walls of sandstone rock.

Turn right at the junction on the hilltop, Quarr Cross, and then fork right almost immediately. This attractive path winds round the hillside and you are now overlooking Bridport. This is Quarr Lane and it brings you back to the main road.

Cross the A 35 to the tarred road opposite. Don't go up the road with "Stop" painted on the tarmac but take the right fork. Then branch almost immediately left along a dirt track that climbs up the middle of Eype Down. These slopes are overgrown with gorse and bracken and are smothered in May with bluebells and later numerous foxgloves. At the top of the first hill you pass a prehistoric burial mound. Contin ahead on the well-marked track and skirt round the next ridge.

Be careful not to take any of the paths that descend the hill towards Bridport. The correct path will bring you out on the top of Eype Down and give views of the valleys on both sides and more distant views from Portland to Lyme Regis. Aim for the highest point on the cliffs in front.

Climb over the locked gate that blocks the path where it passes alongside a sycamore wood. Continue along the hedgerow and you will find yourself going over a stile into National Trust land. Walk

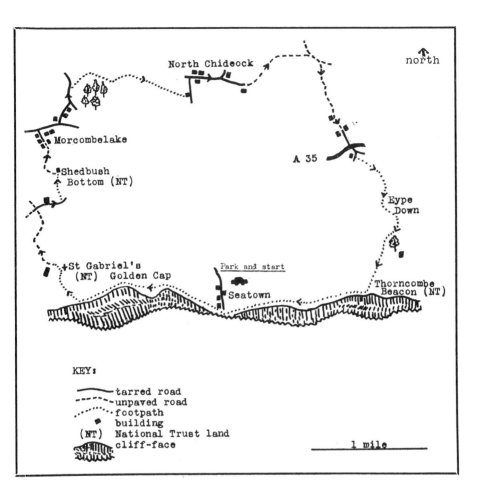

North Chideock

north

Morcombelake

A 35

Shedbush
Bottom (NT)

Eype
Down

+St Gabriel's
(NT) Golden Cap

Park and start

Seatown

Thorncombe
Beacon (NT)

KEY:

———— tarred road
- - - - unpaved road
..........footpath
• building
(NT) National Trust land
cliff-face

1 mile

beside a huge Bronze Age round barrow and up to the summit of Thorncombe Beacon. This, rather than Golden Cap, was the mediaeval beacon point and it was fortified in 1940 with a pillbox, concealed in the clifftop at a height of 507 feet above the sea below. That war relic was blown up by the National Trust in a misguided application of the standards of suburban tidiness above a sense of history.

Turn your back on Bridport and walk along the cliff path for a mile into Seatown. Numerous rabbits have burrows just below the tops of these sandy and inaccessible cliffs. The path drops down into the car-park. ☐

35

Golden stone and thatch of the rustic
farmyard, dating from 1700, at Shedbush
Bottom. It, like all the southern half of
this walk, is on the National Trust's
Golden Cap estate.

The cliff path
at war.

Opposite: Seatown and Golden Cap
in summer 1940; a rare photograph
published at the time with caption
'somewhere on the Scottish coast' to
imply that all Britain was behind
barbed wire. Source: Rodney Legg
collection.

Burton Cliff
and Shipton Gorge

Distance: 7 miles.
Difficult bits: None.
State of paths: Good; generally dry in summer.
Scenery: Varied, with lush valleys and sandy yellow cliffs owned by the National Trust, at the far westerly end of the great Chesil Beach.
Historical interest: St Martin's church, at Shipton Gorge; old stone stiles; West of England's oldest flax-swingling mill.
Natural history: Buzzard country, like most of these walks; reasonable flora on the mixed soils; moorhen and duck; house martins and swallows nesting in the villages in summer.

THE SANDY yellow cliffs at the west end of the Chesil Beach are the starting point for this pleasant *six* mile walk around Burton Bradstock. The stone and thatch cottages of the old village are huddled behind the first line of seaside hills, in contrast to modern bungalows and caravans that advance in a pincer movement towards the shore. The National Trust owns the largest cliff and prevents them meeting.

Behind the village, however, the countryside is largely uninhabited and crossed by a number of tracks and paths, mostly dry and with only one slope that has to be climbed. The next centre of population, at Shipton Gorge, avoids coastal excesses.

A lush valley leads back towards Burton Bradstock, where a west Dorset chalk stream, the Bride, finally assumes the proportions of a river. Across it stands the first flax

mill to be built in the west of England, a reminder that this used to be a working landscape.

Burton Bradstock is on the B3157 coast road from Bridport to Weymouth, three miles east of Bridport.

Park and start in the National Trust car park at the east end of Burton Bradstock, on the extreme edge of the village as you come into it from the Abbotsbury direction. To find the car park you turn south off the main road opposite a thatched cottage that has the number 93 on its door. You drive into a road lined with dormer bungalows, signposted: "To beach and car park".
At the end of the road you pass a National Trust "no parking" sign and drive into a car park.

Walk down to the beach and turn right. The path climbs on to the cliffs. You can walk along the

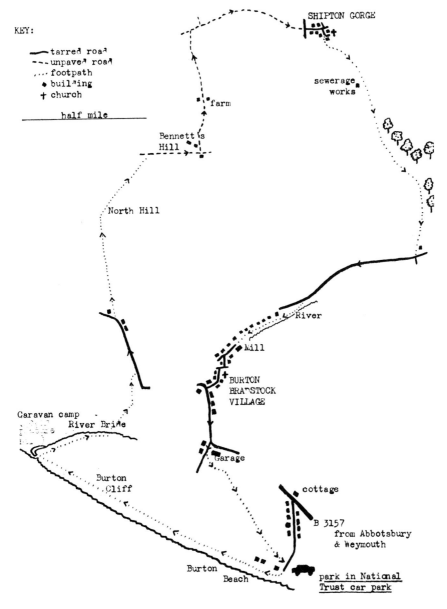

KEY:

────── tarred road
─ ─ ─ unpaved road
,..... footpath
● building
✝ church

half mile

SHIPTON GORGE

sewerage
works

farm

Bennett's
Hill

North Hill

River

Mill

BURTON
BRADSTOCK
VILLAGE

Caravan camp ·
River Bride

Garage

Burton
Cliff

cottage

B 3157
from Abbotsbury
& Weymouth

Burton
Beach

park in National
Trust car park

beach, if you prefer, but the fine shingle is hardly walkable.

Continue for a mile, until a vast valley caravan camp comes into sight. Here you walk down to the **beach. At the first patch of shingle you turn right, over a stile into a field.** Walk straight ahead. Keep the fence and the river to your left. The path bends around the foot of a hill

until Burton village and church come into view. You pass the concrete bases of three wartime Nissen huts.

When you reach the concrete base of a fourth hut, you turn left and cross a footbridge. Follow the right-hand fence to the end of the field. Walk into the next field and turn leftward, keeping the main part of the village to your right, and head gradually uphill beside the left-hand fence towards the two houses and a bungalow in the middle distance. At the end of the field you go through a wooden gate and walk straight ahead to the next gate that is facing you. Walk up a flight of steps on to the main road.

Turn left and walk up the hill, keeping on the right-hand side of the road. You pass a house called "Essendon". Just after this is the drive to a bungalow known as "Culmore'. Thirty-five paces after the drive you come to a pair of metal gates close to a walled garden. But make sure you do not go through an earlier metal gate, which has a "trespassers" notice on it.

The public path runs uphill, from the double gates, beside the walled garden and on to North Hill. The main stretch of the path runs between two hedgerows. Near the top, you have a view of West Bay, and

Lyme Regis beyond. You go through an iron gate and then follow the right-hand fence to the top of North Hill.

At the corner of the field you continue straight ahead, across an old combination of iron and wooden gates. From here the view is over the Marshwood Vale, to the line of peaks (from left to right) of Lambert's Castle, Sliding Hill, Pilsdon Pen and Lewesdon.

The path goes diagonally across the centre of the field and you aim a little to the left of Shipton Hill, which is the squat one looking like the hull of an upturned boat. You go through a gate on to a stony track.

Turn right and walk along this lane. After a quarter of a mile it becomes a tarred road and you come to a ruined barn. A sign says "Pitfold".

Here you turn left, down an unmade track, ignoring an offshoot to the left which is someone's drive. In the dip you pass between a couple of barns and then keep on the lane to the top of the hill. Over the brow, the track goes downhill and then bends to the right. You keep on the main track, and ignore two other paths that branch off to the left.

You are now heading directly towards Shipton Hill, with its white Ordnance Survey pillar showing as a speck on top. Follow the track downhill to the village of Shipton Gorge. You come to a junction at the edge of the village.

Cross straight over towards the church. Turn right along the tarred road that leads up to St Martin's church. At the top of the slope you continue straight ahead, through an iron gate beside the Parish Hall.

Keep to the left in this field, around the back of the hall, to a second gate in about thirty yards. Walk diagonally across this next field to the far corner. You cross earthworks that mark the mediaeval site of the village. In the bottom of the field, about twenty yards from the corner, you will find under the trees an ancient stone stile and footbridge. Walk straight ahead across the next field to an iron gate facing you, and keep the stream and village sewerage works to your right.

Then continue straight ahead across to the bottom of the dip, by the oak trees, and re-cross the stream. Turn left and keep the fence and stream immediately to your left. After about a hundred yards the path goes through an iron gate and crosses back over the stream. In this field you turn right, keeping the stream on your right this time, and walk towards the wood that is facing you.

Before reaching the wood you cross the stream once more, over a stone footbridge. You then come to a stile, go over it, and turn left. Keep the wood immediately to your left and walk along the floor of the valley. Follow the wood into the next field, the path crossing another bridge, this time one with railway sleepers next to a slab of mossy stone.

At the end of this field you leave the edge of the wood, go through an iron gate, and walk along the right-hand side of the next field, following the stream. In the corner of this field you cross the stream by stepping stones and go through an iron gate. Keep following the stream, which is now on your left. At the end of the field you go through an iron gate and pass to the right of a bungalow. You then come to a tarred road.

Turn right and walk into Burton Bradstock, which is a mile away. Just as you approach the first buildings at the edge of the village, close to an old stone bridge, there is a prominent black and white painted "Public footpath" sign on the left. **Beyond it is a stile and you cross this to walk beside the River Bride.** At the end of the path you come into the older part of the village, and pass the Mill House with its historic inscription: "This flax-fwingling mill, the first introduced into the west of England, was erected by Richard Roberts, 1803." About four thousand acres of west Dorset grew flax in the early 19th century. William Stevenson wrote: "The swingling-mills work in a horizontal position; the flax is held by hand against the edge of a board at openings in a frame not unlike that which surrounds the millstones in corn-mills, and is struck by the scutchers, or pieces of wood which project on all sides from a vertical shaft, that is made to revolve very swiftly. By this means the internal parts of the stalk are broken to pieces, and in a great measure separated from the flax."

After the mill, the path is tarred and brings you into Grove Road. Turn left along Darby Lane. On reaching Church Street you turn right, and then turn left into Mill Street, which brings you to the main road. **Turn left along the main road. At the corner, by Cheney's Garage, you continue straight ahead, up Cliff Road.** Immediately after the garage, thirty yards along this road on the left, there is a flight of steps leading to a stone stile. A path brings you to the top of the field. You walk diagonally across the centre. At the far side you cross the remains of a stile and head towards the piece of sea that is visible between the cliffs and the buildings. Midway along the stone wall facing you is another stile. Cross this and walk down to your car. □

Abbotsbury's coast and hills

Distance: 7 miles.
Difficult bits: None.
State of paths: Generally good and easy to find.
Scenery: Magnificent rolling countryside between the Chesil Beach and the Dorset Downs, from which there is one of the classic views of southern England, along the pebble bank to Portland.
Historical interest: Bishop's Limekiln; St Catherine's Chapel; views over the rest of the Abbotsbury monastic complex; Abbotsbury Sub-tropical Gardens; Abbotsbury (Strangways) Castle; Coastguard cottages; Abbotsbury (Iron Age) Castle and hut-circles; Bronze Age burial mounds on Wears Hill.
Natural history: Deer; swans; exotic and rare plants in the Sub-tropical Gardens; native maritime plants.

IN SEVEN MILES of hilly walking country around Abbotsbury you come across some of the best-loved coastal panoramas in Dorset. The scenery is also richly scattered with ruins and relics from all periods, from Iron Age huts to a 19th century limekiln. The scenery is full of variety, lush vegetation and many wild places. Only a quarter of a mile from the beach crowds along the Chesil it is often completely deserted. There are more deer than people. All the paths are unobstructed and easy to follow, in a layout that has changed since the last Ordnance maps were printed as a paths rationalisation scheme has now come into operation on the Strangways estate.

Abbotsbury is on the B 3157 coast road midway between Weymouth and Bridport. Turn north from it into the back road opposite the Post Office in the centre of Abbotsbury village and then follow this road — which goes uphill in the direction of the Hardy Monument. The road is known as Hands Lane at the village end but becomes Bishops Road.

Park half a mile along this road, on the left, in the Bishop's Limekiln Picnic Area. The kiln, at least a hundred years old, is typical of the many scattered across the Dorset Downs which until ˙ the 1920s produced building mortar, soil dressings and limewash. A diagram shows how the kiln was filled from the top with layers of chalk alternating with wood or coal, the slow combustion converting the chalk into quicklime. **Walk along the road downhill back into Abbotsbury, along Hands Lane,** to the main road. Walk along the street to the right-hand end of the Post Office block of buildings. Then turn left, along the gravel track, beside the notice to St Catherine's Chapel. The

Bishop's Limekiln produced mortar, soil dressings and limewash. The walk starts from here. Photograph: John Pitfield.

chapel path is straight ahead, and is a diversion from the main route of this walk. It is worth the uphill walk, not only for the chapel itself but for the superb view over the entire Abbotsbury monastic complex, from the ruins to the Tithe Barn and the Swannery. The chapel, built late in the 14th century, is on an oval platform at the top of the hill and was also part of the Benedictine abbey. St Catherine is a typical high-place dedication to the patron saint of spinsters. Women in search of a husband prayed here for "A husband, St. Catherine. A handsome one, St Catherine. A rich one, St Catherine. A nice one, St Catherine. And soon, St Catherine." After the dissolution of the abbey in 1539 the chapel was retained as a sea-mark, and repaired in 1742. The ceiling was restored in the 1970s, and other repairs were also made using the same bright yellow local stone. Spiral stairs lead to the octagonal turret beside the roof. A door opens on to a balcony, around the side of the roof, which was used for a sea-watch.

After you have seen the chapel walk back down the hill along the same path, towards the village, to the barns. Turn left after the kissing gate. The track leads to a junction with another sandy track and here you turn left. Follow it, passing Rose Cottage and a thatched cottage beside the cricket pitch. It leads down a valley to the Chesil Beach.

Fork right at the first wooden signpost, on to the track towards the back of the beach. Continue straight ahead along the path to the beach. There is a car-park to the right.

After about 300 yards a road joins the beach track, from Abbotsbury Sub-tropical Gardens. You continue along the beach track, which from here is tarred. Clumps of thrift and campion

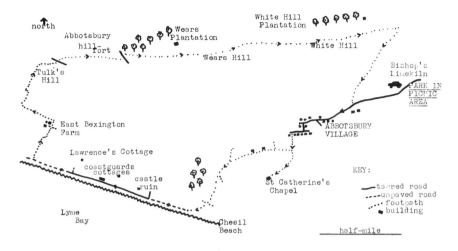

north

Abbotsbury hill-fort

Tulk's Hill

East Bexington Farm

Lawrence's Cottage

coastguards cottages
castle ruin

Lyme Bay

Wears Plantation

Wears Hill

White Hill Plantation

White Hill

Bishop's Limekiln

PARK IN PICNIC AREA

ABBOTSBURY VILLAGE

St Catherine's Chapel

Chesil Beach

KEY:

— tarred road
- - - unpaved road
· · · · · footpath
▪ building

half-mile

Overleaf: St Catherine's Chapel and its hill, with the Chesil Beach and Portland as the backdrop to one of the most famous views in southern England, photographed by Frederick G. Masters. The close-up photograph is by Colin Graham.

grow at the edge of the pebbles during the summer months. The road passes beneath a stone wall on the hill, behind which on the west side stand the ruins of Abbotsbury Castle which was destroyed by fire in 1912. You then pass a farmstead and a line of former coastguard cottages. A third of a mile after these you pass the track to Lawrence's Cottage.

Nearly half a mile after this you come to a black-painted iron gate. Turn right through it, along the grass track beside a field, to Bexington Farm — cream walls and slate roof — about a third of a mile away. On the left of the track, facing towards Portland, the farmer has kindly provided a rustic seat. At the top of the field the path goes through an iron gate and passes immediately to the right of the farm's asbestos barns. After the buildings it bends to the left, and brings you into a field. Go through this gate and continue to the next in 50 yards. **Follow the left hand edge of this arable**

field, to a stile midway along the second side. Turn right in this pasture, and now keep the hedgerow to your right. You cross into a wild hillside which along with the first pasture came into National Trust ownership in 1979 as part of a holding surrounding Labour-in-Vain Farm. Follow the hedgerow uphill. At the top of the field you follow the boundary fence around to the right. **This brings you to the main road. Cross to the hunting gate beside the stone wall on the other side.** The path then climbs on to the nearest corner of Abbotsbury Castle, a double-banked Iron Age hill-fort of about 50 BC, and you follow the southern rampart overlooking the coast road and the sea. Inside it are the best preserved prehistoric hut circles in Dorset, their walls about 30 feet in diameter with entrances facing away from the prevailing wind. At the next corner of the fort you drop down to a lane.

Cross to the stile on the other side and walk straight ahead on to the summit of the hill. This is Wears Hill, and once again you have that remarkable view over the Fleet and Chesil Beach to Portland. You pass several prehistoric burial mounds and a Royal Observer Corps "ping-station" — a room about 15 feet by eight feet, plus toilet, 20 feet deep — constructed for radiation monitoring.

At the end of the field, after a corrugated-roofed reservoir, you go through a gate on the summit of the hill into an arable field. Follow the right-hand edge. Just to the left of the far corner there is an iron gate into the next field.

Go through this and follow the fence line, which is now on your left. At the end of the field you come to three iron gates and go through the right-hand one. Keep the fence to your left. At the end of the field is a stile, which you cross, and then go immediately through an iron gate.

Turn right, across the centre of the field between the escarpment and White Hill Plantation. At the end of the field a bridleway signpost shows a sharp right turn heading towards the sea, aiming towards the Swannery and the Tithe Barn at Abbotsbury to be more precise. At the edge of the hill you walk down a deep-cut trackway. The Tithe Barn is the large thatched building at the left-hand edge of Abbotsbury village. After the lynchets you go through a hunting gate and follow the fence downhill. Continue along the fence until you emerge on a tarred road, above three modern barns.

Turn left along the road, uphill past Oxlip Coppice. The limekiln parking place is just around the next corner.

□

Langton Herring and the Fleet

Distance: 8 miles.

Difficult bits: Short stretch of main road walking with two blind bends and fast cars liable to appear at any moment – you are warned in the text that this is a case where it is hazardous to walk towards oncoming traffic.

State of paths: Good and well marked.

Scenery: Beautiful, if a little tame by Dorset standards, the landlocked Fleet lagoon having only ripples and the inland countryside being pleasantly rural but rather undramatic.

Historical interest: Wartime range where the Dambusting bouncing bomb was tested.

Natural history: Major bird reserve for shelduck, tern and heron; beds of oyster shells, millions of years old; Alexanders, a monastery pot-herb, invading hedgerows.

BEHIND THE Chesil Bank, and its shallow salt-water lake, is one of the lusher dairylands of Dorset. Between the quiet shore and the chalk hills that make the skyline from Abbotsbury to Ridgeway is a slice of moderately undulating countryside with small woods and a scattering of thatched cottages.

The waters of the Fleet are the county's finest all-weather bird reserve, with the pebble ridges of the Chesil Bank taking the sea's frontline battering. Ripples are the most that its lagoon can usually manage, at least on a summer afternoon.

The starting point for this *eight* mile walk is the tightly clustered village of Langton Herring. It lies just to the south of the main B3157 coast road from Weymouth to Bridport, midway between Weymouth and Abbotsbury. Langton Herring is sheltered from the weather and concealed from the main road by a dense surround of tall trees. Below, an annual weed gives some of its hedgerows a Mediterranean green in early summer. Alexanders, a former monastery pot-herb, is rampant around the village and exceeds five feet by the middle of the year, before dying back to brown stalks loaded with dry seeds.

In following the sign to "Langton Herring" off the B3157, two miles west of Chickerell, you also follow the green-painted sign to the "Elm Tree Inn". As you come into the village, turn left at the telephone kiosk, where the signs are to "Village and Coastguards" and also to the "Elm Tree Inn".

A short distance down this road is the Elm Tree Inn, and you park in its grass paddock immediately to the right of the main pub buildings. Do not block the tarmac area but leave your car on the grassed area. Permission for us to leave cars here has

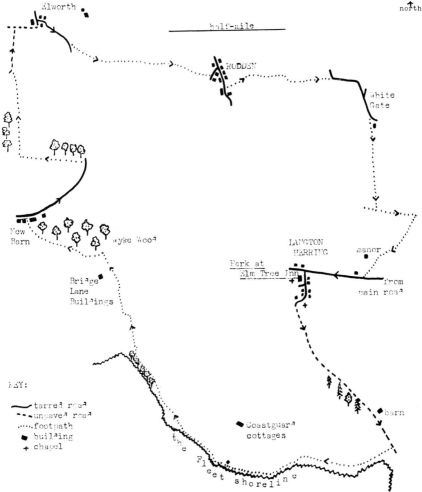

KEY:

- tarred road
- unpaved road
- footpath
- ■ building
- + chapel

half-mile

Elworth

RODDEN

White Gate

New Barn

Wyke Wood

LANGTON HERRING manor

Park at Elm Tree Inn

from main road

Bridge Lane Buildings

Coastguard cottages

barn

the Fleet shoreline

been given by the publicans, Derek and Carol Ross, so please give them a little business in return when you come back thirsty and hungry. It is a pub that sets high standards, with first-rate ploughman's lunches and a dependable range of food. Check a blackboard at the bar for the meals of the day.

Leave the Elm Tree by the main entrance, the one through which you arrived, and turn right. Then con-tinue straight ahead along the "No through road". You pass cottages, a bungalow and two council houses (but if you find you are passing the parish church you have missed a turn). Follow the road around a corner, passing the small Methodist chapel, built in 1909.

After the chapel the track bends to the left, with a signpost "Footpath Fleet 1". This track gives you a view over the Fleet and Chesil Beach,

Observing the wildfowl from a punt.

and then runs to the left of a small wood. At the bottom of the slope there is a barn.

A hundred yards after the barn, on your right, there is a gate and stile into a field, and the signboard "Coastal path". Take this path and walk along the edge of the field, beside the Fleet lagoon. This shoreline is often alive with dunlin and other waders. Further out, you can usually spot shelduck, tern and herons. After about half a mile you pass an anchorage for small rowing boats. Concrete-filled prototypes of wartime Dambuster-type bouncing bombs have been found on this beach, and one object that might have been one is lying by the water. The cliffs, though only a few feet high, are entirely composed of grey layers of crushed oyster shells, several millions of years old.

Follow the shore around this miniature headland and then walk up to the edge of the field, shortly before you reach two stunted fir trees. The path now follows the left-hand edge of the field. At the end of the field you cross some fence posts by a stone wall, and are now facing inland towards the Hardy Monument. **Keep the trees immediately to your left and walk along the foot of the valley.** At the end of the field there

is a kissing gate and you continue straight ahead through it, keeping the hedgerow and a ditch to your left. You then come to two stiles with a short stretch of grass between them.

Cross the first stile but not the second — you turn left, after about forty paces. Here, by the stream, is a signpost: "Coastal path". Cross the stream and turn right, towards a yellow-stone house and farmyard. Make sure you keep to the same side of the stream as the farm, and do not stray back across a second bridge. The public footpath signposted "Coastal path" runs to the right of Bridge Lane Buildings, towards Wyke Wood.

On reaching the trees you turn left (leaving the "Coastal path" route) and follow the outside edge of the wood uphill to the farm and cottages at New Barn. Walk through the farmyard.

Turn right and walk along the tarred road for about half a mile until you come to a wood on the left-hand side. Turn left and follow the side of this wood, and the hedgerow, until you reach a second block of woodland. Turn right on reaching this wood.

It is called Hodders Coppice and you keep it immediately to your left as you head towards the ridge of

hills. At the top, on Merry Hill, the footpath joins a farm track and heads towards the main range of chalk hills to the left of Portesham village.

It then drops down a steep, stony slope and you turn right at the bottom, into the hamlet of Elworth. Turn right at the centre of the farmstead, after the sheepdog kennels and opposite the Old Farm House. You pass a bungalow and go through an iron gate ("Please shut the gate"). This road is tarred and climbs a slope.

At the top, after passing between two electricity poles, you turn off to the left, through a wooden gate. Walk slightly to the right of centre across this field, following a well marked bank.

You keep to the top of this ridge and continue straight ahead through four iron gates, bringing the distance to about a mile. You then drop into Rodden. The path emerges at the foot of the hill, in front of a timber chalet and to the right of the greystone house with classical lines.

Turn left along the tarred road, and then right at the signpost "Langton Herring 1¼". After about a hundred yards, just before the slate-roofed Rodden Farm House, you turn left through a metal gate. A dirt cattle track runs across a couple of fields and then follows the right-hand hedgerow around the third field. The next stretch is an old green lane between dense hedgerows, and the track then follows the right-hand hedge across a field beside the main Portesham to Weymouth road.

On reaching the road you turn right and walk around the corner, but be careful as though this is only a short piece of main road walking it is along one that has a high accident record. You have to walk around two blind bends. While in general it is safer to walk towards oncoming traffic, it is not in this case as many of the cars corner at speed and have shaved the nearside bank. Always ensure you can be seen, and have a way of escape.

On the other side of the double bend there is a straight length of road, with a signpost at White Gate and a modern stone house at the next corner. Here, on the right-hand side, you turn right just before you reach the house — through a scotch gate between two sets of hazard arrows. Follow the left-hand edge of the field, behind the back garden of the house. The field drops into a dip and you then climb to the top of the hill, keeping in a straight line. At the top of the hill, in the corner of the field, you slip under the wire and come into an arable field. Turn left and follow the hedgerow to the pine trees at the end of the next field.

As you approach these, turn abruptly right and walk downhill diagonally across this field, aiming for the metal gate in the opposite corner. This is the lowest corner of the field, near an old walled garden, and you are heading towards the nearest glimpse of the sea. Langton Herring lies behind the trees in front of you.

After going through the gate you keep the hedgerow to your left for about 200 feet and then go through another iron gate. Walk directly ahead towards the trees, across a small sheep pasture, to the wooden gate facing you. A track then climbs the hill.

At the top you come to a tarred road and turn right. This brings you into the vilage, and the first left takes you back to your car and the Elm Tree inn. □

Powerstock
and South Poorton

Distance: 4 miles.

Difficult bits: None.

State of paths: Damp sections, rubber boots advisable other than in a drought.

Scenery: Wild, deep-cut valleys, the quintessential landscape of Devon-in-Dorset.

Historical interest: 1840 school; West Milton church ruin; South Poorton church; Powerstock church; Kenneth Allsop's grave.

Natural history: Hawks, buzzards, foxs, deer; high possibility of disturbing something interesting.

REAL EXPLORERS' country is penetrated in this four mile walk. It centres on the yellow stone village of Powerstock in the gathering hills at the edge of west Dorset's Marshwood Vale, to the east of the road between Bridport and Beaminster. This is the point where the landscape changes into what is not typically Dorset. Minority Dorset, this was, until popularity and new colonists followed publicity towards the end of the 1960s. It is at last accepted that Dorset has three distinct types of scenery — downland, heathland, and Powerstock country. Its western essence is summed up in a secret valley with no name which captures the character of the region and its quickly changing, Devonian landscape. It goes for over a mile without a single building which, even in these wilds, is unusual. Here is the most dependable country in Dorset for seeing foxes and buzzards.

Overhead, frequently harassed by crows, the buzzards circle and mew, sometimes in family groups. For all it offers, the walk is not overly strenuous and the rough country is crossed by level tracks, though gumboots are necessary.

Park and start in the centre of Powerstock village. There is a relatively wide stretch of road beneath the church wall on the lane that leads towards the Three Horsehoes and Eggardon Hill.

Walk to the crossroads below the church wall and take the minor road on the opposite side, between two thatched cottages, signposted with a wooden post: "West Milton 1." After a hundred yards the track bends to the left around an old school building and then turns fully to the left as you reach the hedgerow. Walk up to the iron gate and then ahead into the field.

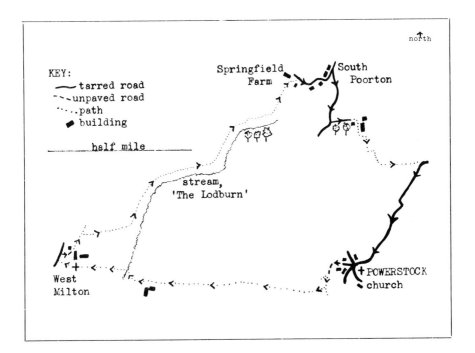

KEY:
- tarred road
- unpaved road
- path
- building

half mile

Springfield Farm

South Poorton

stream, 'The Lodburn'

West Milton

POWERSTOCK church

north

Forty paces later there is a fork and you take the left of the two tracks, still going ahead but slightly downhill. After a further 70 paces, just after you pass the ivy-covered wall of a ruined building, there is a small triangular clearing with a view to the opposite side of the valley.

From here another path branches off, to the right. Take this and continue straight ahead along the side of the valley, walking a well-defined path which after a mile passes between dense hedgerows and brings you to an iron gate.

Keep walking ahead, towards the first electricity pole. The path follows the terrace in the hillside, above the slope from the stream. At the end of this terrace there is a wooden gate and the buildings of West Milton are in sight.

Keep walking ahead along the track, which now follows a fence.

The track continues straight ahead along the right-hand side of the farm, beside the oak tree. After the tree there is a gate and the path then continues ahead.

Thirty paces later it turns to the right and goes downwards between a hedge and wire fence. At the bottom there is a bridge and a small wooden gate.

Go through the gate and ahead uphill, aiming just to the left of the barn on the skyline. The path brings you into West Milton's old churchyard. As for the church, there is only a tower as the rest was demolished in the 1840s, most of the stone being used to build Powerstock school. Today the result is a restful walled garden with grass and table-tombs, facing straight up the alley to the prehistoric ramparts on Eggardon Hill. The surviving tower is 15th century and the building,

53

technically a chapel though in appearance a village church, was dedicated to St Mary Magdalene.

Leave the churchyard through the iron gate by the tower and walk downhill to the tarred road. Turn right for forty paces and then turn right again, into a farm signposted: "Bridleway, Ridgeback Lane 1". This bends to the left between the farm buildings and then passes two high hedgebanks. Fifty yards after the beginning of the hedgerows there is a wide gap on the right-hand side with a gate.

Go through this gate and ahead into the field. Walk diagonally across the field to the far left-hand corner which is at the top of a steep slope. You are now overlooking one of the wildest valleys in Dorset, with bracken sides, dense tree cover at the bottom, and marsh plants around hillside springs. At this corner of the field there is a gap in the hedge and the path continues ahead. It runs along the left-hand side of the valley, about a hundred yards to the

left of the stream, known as the "Lodburn". The path can be picked up again at the opposite side of the next field by the gaps and remains of gates in the hedges. If you have any difficulty, walk down towards the stream but remember not to cross it — the path follows the stream, about a hundred yards to the left of it, for a mile. It is relatively simple.

One field is completely abandoned to bracken. At the end of the next field there is a gate and the path now continues ahead, following the left-hand hedgerow. Next you follow the hillside slightly to the left as the stream changes direction. At the end of the field the path follows a hedgerow, on your right.

Do not follow the hedgerow as it veers to the left, away from the main valley bottom, but look out for three bars of wood in the hedge. Climb over these fence posts, through the hedge, towards a beech wood on the far bank of the stream. Still keep the stream on your right, and after a

54

Opposite: West Milton, photographed by Rodney Legg. Above: Looking back on Powerstock from the first section of path.

ton Hill only."

Turn left along this road, past a timber rack for milkchurns, to the end of the tarred section. Here there is a bungalow and a thatched cottage.

The footpath branches off to the right, passing between the cottage and an asbestos barn, then through a metal gate immediately to the right of the cottage garden. After the cottage garden the path turns to the left through a black painted gate, and then turns abruptly right along a grass path between two clipped hazel hedgerows. This sounds intricate, but the owner of the cottage has made the path easily followable with yellow pointers, and had even run his electric mower over the first hundred yards of the old cattle drove leading away from the cottage. It is the best example of kindness towards walkers we have come across.

At the end of the cut section the drove turns to the left, and then to the right, emerging at an iron gate. On the other side there is an arable field.

Walk along the left-hand edge of the field to a green gate and on to the tarred road. Turn right. Walk for a mile along this road, back into Powerstock village. As the road finally drops into the village there is a gate on the left into the churchyard. Just inside, on the left, there is a stone to author and naturalist Kenneth Allsop who died in 1973. Behind it, now in fruit, is a medlar. It was one of Kenneth's favourite trees and he had obtained this specimen for his mill home at West Milton shortly before he died. Inside the church tower there are pictures and notes on its history in a well-run museum section which other churches could copy. □

hundred yards you will find a track running by the left side of a hedgerow, some 75 yards to the left of the stream. This path gradually becomes a recognisable track and goes through an iron gate.

You then walk uphill along a cattle path between two hedgerows and a small stream. The track reaches a gate and farmyard, called Springfield Farm. You do not go through the gate but turn to the right, passing beside the rear of the sheds, and emerge onto the tarred road by a stile.

Turn right along the tarred road walk into the hamlet of South Poorton. After the second thatched cottage another road comes sharply uphill from the right.

Turn right into this deep-cut lane. The road passes a farmhouse and then climbs the other side of the valley, where there is a sign "Poor-

Askerswell
and Eggardon

Distance: 5 miles.
Difficult bits: None, apart from a couple of hill climbs.
State of paths: Damp in places, water-proof footwear sensible for most
of the year.
Scenery: Breathtaking as you climb from the vale on to the chalk
massif, with its view to Dartmoor and Start Point.
Historical interest: Vernacular architecture at North Eggardon Farm;
Eggardon hill-fort – south half owned by the National Trust; Askerswell
church; village pound.
Natural history: Hawks, buzzards, butterflies, chalkland flowers.

THE ESCARPMENTS and coombes of Eggardon are the westward extremity of the chalk land-mass of southern England. Below, for the last twelve miles of Dorset, the landscape is pure Devon. This walk of just under *five miles* covers the scenic divide where the landscape changes. All the way there are views —and from the 800 foot heights of Eggardon itself they widen to a skyline that runs from Start Point across Dartmoor. For many this is the finest countryside in Dorset and the Iron Age hill-fort of Eggardon makes a setting unequalled in British archaeology.

Eggardon is maimed on the same scale as Dorchester's Maiden Castle with waves of stout ramparts. They must also have held out with slingstones against the Roman legionaries at the climax of the onslaught on the West after the invasion of 43 AD. The southern half of the fort, scaled in this walk, is deeply pockmarked with circles where thatched huts stood and grain was stored. Six of the holes are said to have been added by a German bomber returning from Bristol and unloading before crossing the Channel.

In the northern interior of Eggardon the archaeological evidence has been destroyed by a cabbage patch; kale can unfortunately flourish on this most windswept of summits. But the turf of the surrounding prehistoric banks is still alive with butterflies. A checklist, by lepidopterist Michael Murless, has 31 species and most are abundant: "I think Eggardon is on a fairly strong migration route and it is here that I always see the first migrants of the year, and always in a particular spot".

Equally, there are the birds. Sunday Times reporter Brian Jackman, who has a cottage in the hill's shadow at Powerstock, can listen on

Park and start beside the A35 below the Askers Motel.

Eggardon to all the birds of west Dorset. It is bird-of-prey country and Jackman reels off descriptions of buzzards, hen harriers, sparrowhawks, kestrels and what to him is the finest and most thrilling sight of all—"the sickle-winged hobby, our smallest falcon and our most beautiful, a peregrine in miniature with a fondness for high-speed acrobatics".

In a storm sky the view from Eggardon's precipice is breathtaking. Weather is important for your walking too, but remember that even on dry days some of the water from the chalk emerges as springs in the foothills crossed by this walk. So waterproof footwear is sensible at all times except drought.

Park and start in the A35 layby between Askers Motel and the Travellers Rest (four miles on the Dorchester side of Bridport) beside blue RAC **Box number 292.**

Walk downhill along the main road keeping to the right-hand verge. You are overlooking Askerswell village and church.

On your right, just before the "Dual carriageway ahead" sign there is a wooden stile in the hedgerow.

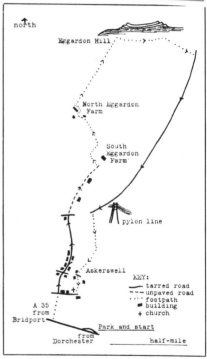

north

Eggardon Hill

North Eggardon Farm

South Eggardon Farm

pylon line

Askerswell

A 35 from Bridport

from Dorchester

Park and start

KEY:
— tarred road
- - - unpaved road
···· footpath
▪ building
+ church

half-mile

Cross this and walk downhill through the iron gate at the foot of the scarp. Continue straight ahead to the metal gate by the elm tree at the road junction (to the left of the farm buildings).

Keep ahead in the same direction along the tarred road signposted

Opposite: The Eggardon massif from the vale. Photograph: Rodney Legg. Above: The Iron Age ramparts on top of the hill, designed for slingstone warfare. This half of the fort is a National Trust property. It has spectacular views over the Marshwood Vale and into Devon. Photograph: C. Bubb.

"Askerswell". Walk over the cross-roads in the village and uphill in the direction of "Spyway". In contrast to its cottages, the last Askerswell building has an inscribed slab "Legg's Mead, AD 1943" and is a hideously undesigned row of council houses with the best view in the village.

Continue straight ahead over the crossroads at the top of the hill. This "Private Road" is a public bridleway that brings you into the basin below Eggardon Hill and its associated massif of the Bell Stone outcrops. Across this road the 160-foot pylons stride down the slope and proceed in single file across the Marshwood Vale.

Walk past the first group of farm buildings, and then past a pair of cottages. On the left, just after the second telegraph pole from this building, there is a hunting gate in the corner of the field. Inside the gate there is a cattle trough and sycamore tree.

Go through this gate and follow the hedgerow downhill through a second gate to the stream. Cross the water and follow the bank upstream to another hunting gate. Open this, cross a smaller stream, and then turn in a leftward direction up the bank. There is a gap in the hedge.

59

Enter this field and follow the left-hand hedge. Do not go through the gate by the transformer post but continue uphill for 40 paces to a second gate. Walk towards the farmhouse, which is the right-hand of the group of buildings on the skyline. Go through the gate and follow the stony track into the farmyard. Skirt round the barn. This building is an amazing amalgam of sarsen boulders, Ham-stone ashlars, chalk blocks, and bricks at the corners.

Continue along the wall to the end of the farm buildings and then fork right so that you are facing two gates. Take the right-hand of the pair. Follow the track along the left hedgerow and climb to the hunting gate at the entrance to the south slope of Eggardon.

Walk ahead a short distance, then turn to the right and climb up an old deep-cut trackway. At the top you are among the complex defences of the eastern entrance to the hill-fort.

Leave the fort at this point, through the wooden gate, and follow the right-hand hedge. The gate at the end brings you out at a tarred road.

Turn right and walk downhill for about a mile. You are overlooking the Marshwood Vale and the country under Eggardon where you have been walking. Look out for the big pylon line which crosses the road.

About 200 paces after you have walked under the pylon line there is a patch of tall scrub in the left-hand hedge. Immediately next to this, in the left hedge, is a gap with fencing. Go through this and follow the right-hand hedge downhill. Open the metal gate at the bottom of the hill and then go through the second gate that faces you, a short distance ahead on the right.

Turn to the left and follow the track down to a gate. Open this gate and turn left along a concrete roadway for about 30 paces to a gap with timber fencing in the right-hand hedge. Go through this and turn in a right-hand direction diagonally across the field to the lower right-hand corner. Walk through the gate in the corner and continue downhill to the lane below the village church.

Cross straight over the tarred road and into the drive of the left-hand of the two new houses. Just a few paces along this drive, on the left, there is a pathway between two hedgerows. It passes to the left of the side wall of the house and climbs uphill to the church between deep fern-covered banks.

At the top, walk into the churchyard. One of the treasures of Askerswell church is a great slab of Purbeck marble, four feet across, which with its partner stone (now at Whitchurch Canonicorum) has an inscription which translated reads: "Sir Thomas de Luda and Lady Alianore his wife lie here: God have mercy on their souls: who gave Holewale to this house". Sir Thomas gave the manor of Holwell, six miles south of Sherborne, to the monks at Abbotsbury in 1320. The donors were probably buried at the Abbey and the stones removed after having been stripped of their brasses by Parliamentary troops in the Civil War.

Turn right on to the road outside the main porch. Walk past Court Farm and the stone-walled village pound to the tree at the corner.

Immediately to the left of the tree there is a metal gate. Go through this and walk directly uphill to the gate at the foot of the ridge. Climb to the stile at the top and turn left to your car, taking care to walk on the right-hand side and towards the oncoming traffic. □

On the Downs

Distance: 7 miles.
Difficult bits: None.
State of paths: Some ploughed cereal fields to skirt around.
Scenery: Rolling uplands with coombes and small woods, typical of Dorset downlands.
Historical interest: Jackman's Cross; Grimstone Down prehistoric settlement and fields.
Natural history: Deer, frequently in some numbers; chalkland flowers on the remaining patches of ancient unimproved turf.

THIS WALK into the heartlands of the Dorset Downs crosses *seven* miles of its least inhabited countryside. It brings you into the unknown territory between the Sydling and Cerne valleys where there is a lost coombe sandwiched by the hills. There is no village and the buildings at Magiston barely qualify as a hamlet. It is simple walking country as there are no severe slopes to climb, or bad obstructions, but stout shoes are needed as you have to cross a couple of arable fields at the beginning before you can embark on the main section of the walk. This is increasingly the penalty of entering what is now typically Dorset, because large blocks of the central hills are agriculturally intensively managed. In a walk such as this you break through into something more basic, but it is impossible to find a completely illusory landscape where nothing appears to have changed in the past hundred years.

Park and start just off the main A37 Dorchester to Yeovil road half a mile north from the point where the A356 branches off to Frampton and Maiden Newton. The place on the A37 you are looking for is a VIP petrol station with a red sign saying "Guaranteed used cars" on the east side of a straight, level section of road.

Turn east off the main road here, on to a lane signposted "Sydling St Nicholas 2¾" and stop almost immediately. Pull off the road on to the grass and park on the wide verge about 25 yards away from the crossroads. The grass here is firm and you are safely away from the visibility splays of the junction, which should not be obstructed. As you leave your car you will see a metal gate into the field on the left-hand side of the lane signposted to Sydling.
Enter this field and walk diagonally

across it, aiming for the left-hand side of the stone barn. This is a public right-of-way.

Forty yards to the left of the barn there is a gap in the hedge and you walk through this, downhill, into the next field. You are heading down into the valley and aim for the second barn from the left. As you approach the lower part of the field you continue towards the main group of farm buildings and continue walking in a straight line, across an old hedgebank into another field. Head slightly to the right of the white-roofed barn.

This brings you to a metal gate and the tarred road, just before you reach the two barns. Turn left along the road for 40 paces and then branch off downhill to the right along the drive signposted "Magiston Farm". The right-of-way follows the tarred drive to the end and then climbs uphill along a flinty track.

Do not climb to the top of the hill but turn into the hillside field to the left of the track. In this sloping field you follow the rough path which is a little below the top edge. Aim to the right of the small wood on the horizon.

Pass between the top of the wood and the hedgebank. As the wood swings outwards to the right, the field narrows, and you finally follow the right-hand hedgerow to the

Park just off the A37 opposite this filling station, by the 'Sydling St Nicholas 2¾' turn.

entrance to the wood. Enter the young plantation and turn to the right. Walk beside the overgrown hedgerow along the right-hand side of the wood. The track climbs gradually uphill, curving to the left and then the right, bringing you out on to a field at the top of the hill.

You cross this field diagonally, to the far left-hand corner. Here there are some wooden bars. Cross on to the farm track which leads directly ahead to the barn on Shearplace Hill. Its main walls are blocks of chalk.

Continue along the track, through a metal gate, and pass a concrete watertank. You leave the field by an iron gate and turn right along another dirt track. *The point should be made that here the legal course of the right-of-way runs through the middle of the field to the right of the path, which at the time of writing is deep in kale. It would seem reasonable to use the track rather than damage the crop, as this is a clear case where a path could be diverted in everyone's interests. Should you agree with us in making your own commonsense decision, remember that you must now be cautious—when you leave the official path you no longer have legal protection, and you have to take*

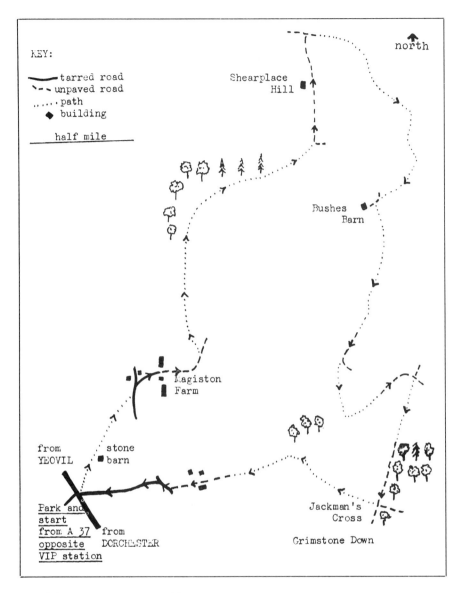

KEY:

⬤— tarred road
`-- unpaved road
...... path
◆ building

half mile

north

Shearplace
Hill

Bushes
Barn

Magiston
Farm

from
YEOVIL

stone
barn

Park and
start
from A 37
opposite
VIP station

from
DORCHESTER

Jackman's
Cross

Grimstone Down

special care not to stumble upon hazards like bulls.

The alternative track in this case continues downhill, through a metal gate, into a coombe. At the foot of this valley it turns to the right and follows the valley bottom, where you once more find yourself walking the legal course of the path. Keep the sheep-fence immediately to your right and walk towards a shepherd's hut.

After passing the corrugated-iron shepherd's hut you go through a

63

metal gate and continue along the bottom of the valley. Because it is without a stream, this three-mile long valley is one of the emptiest in the whole of the Dorset chalklands and can only be reached on foot. Throughout it is grassy and easy to walk. The only buildings are at Bushes Barn and here the path turns to the right, through an iron gate, and then after 30 paces turns to the left through a second gate.

You now follow the right-hand fence and stay in the bottom of the valley. Keep following the fence, slowly going downhill, for more than half a mile. The track now becomes stony and runs along the foot of the hillside. It turns sharply to the left about a quarter of a mile from a wood.

Here you leave the track and go through the gate into the field facing you. Turn to the left and walk diagonally across the field, uphill to the line of electricity poles running along the top side. You go through the iron gate into another piece of downland.

Turn left along a depression in the sloping side of this field. It becomes a chalky track as you near the summit. At the top the track meets two others, but you take neither of these.

Instead you turn abruptly to the right and follow the hedgerow towards the right-hand end of the line of trees on the horizon. Keep the hedgerow to your left and go through the iron gate beside the wood. Continue until a second muddy trackway joins from the left. Here, in a triangle of barbed wire ten feet to the left, is Dorset's saddest wayside monument. There are two stones and one of them was the socket for a mediaeval preaching cross. It is two feet square, with a hole nine inches by

Two flowers in ancient grasslands.

Green-winged orchid

Meadow saxifrage

eleven inches in the centre. Covered with moss, these two stones are all that remains of Jackman's Cross.

From the cross you take none of the well-defined tracks, but go through the wooden gate into the field. Walk ahead, downhill, into the valley. There is a gate, by a cattle-trough, in the fence facing you. From here you aim towards the left-hand end of the wood at the bottom. The rough country to the left is Grimstone Down and the banks you can see mark the field systems of a major prehistoric settlement. It is the best that remains from the time when these entire downlands were occupied by Celtic communities, and Grimstone Down has only survived thanks to the intervention of the Environment Department with a preservation order.

At the foot of the hill there is a wooden gate. You are now on a grassy track between two fields. At the bottom of the valley this becomes a tractor-track through the field, and it leads you to some buildings and then the tarred road.

Turn right, crossing the bridge over the Sydling Water, and then turn left, uphill along the lane signposted "Frampton $\frac{3}{4}$". Your car is at the top of the hill. □

64

Frome St Quintin and Chantmarle

Distance: 6 miles.
Difficult bits: Finding the path in a few places, so keep in mind the 'head for' features mentioned in the text.
State of paths: Damp except in a drought.
Scenery: Undulating countryside below the downland escarpment beside the upper reaches of the River Frome.
Historical interest: Sarsen stone mounting-block; Chantmarle (Police Training College).
Natural history: Foxes, variety of small birds – nothing guaranteed but keep your eyes open.

WHERE THE River Frome trickles through the northern escarpment of the chalk downs, there is some varied countryside. This walk is based on the village of Frome St. Quintin, about ten miles north-west of Dorchester, and covers **six miles**. The scenery is undulating, with some fine views from the higher ground, and cottages of deep-yellow stone tucked away below. It is not an area that is on any of the usual visitor circuits, which enhances its appeal. But if you do the walk at a damp time of the year you will need rubber boots as the valley fields can be muddy. The greatest single attraction is the beauty of Chantmarle, a fine 17th century mansion.

Turn west off the A37 (Yeovil) road about ten miles from Dorchester, at the foot of the long hill after the Clay Pigeon restaurant. Shortly before you reach the crossroads at Holywell, with the Evershot turn-ing, there is a lane signposted to "Frome St.Quintin, Chantmarle". You take this road.

In a mile you come to Frome St. Quintin. Park and start in the centre of the village, on the wide stretch of road beside the big house and opposite the cottages. There is room here either side of the post box (park against the wall so that you do not block the entrances to the cottages).

Start the walk by continuing along the road. One unusual and unre-corded relic on the right-hand side of the road, outside one of the cot-tages, is a one-ton boulder of sarsen stone that has a ledge or step in it. The stone is set against a wall, uti-lising its shape to provide a mount-ing-block for reaching the saddle of a horse.

You pass the phonebox and walk downhill and to the right around

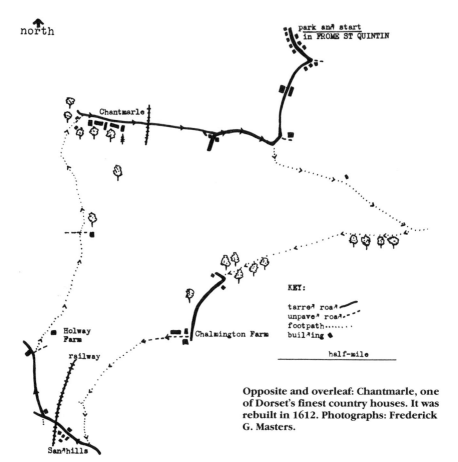

north

park and start
in FROME ST QUINTIN

Chantmarle

KEY:

tarred road
unpaved road
footpath
building ♦

half-mile

Holway
Farm

railway

Chalmington Farm

Sandhills

Opposite and overleaf: Chantmarle, one of Dorset's finest country houses. It was rebuilt in 1612. Photographs: Frederick G. Masters.

the sharp corner at the bottom. The road passes a red-brick terrace, facing a farmyard, and you come to the (back) of the village sign at the end of the village. To the left, a short distance from the road, are some barns.
On the far side of the corner, facing you, are several iron gates into the fields. Take the centre one, straight ahead of you, and walk along a stony trackway. This bends to the left and continues to the top of the hill, in half a mile. You pass a small cattle shelter and continue through a metal gate along the main track. In a quarter of a mile you come to

a second gate, within sound of the A 37 traffic.
Here you turn right, virtually back on yourself, and descend towards the trees in the foot of the coombe. Follow the valley side and keep just to the right of the base of the valley. At the end of the trees you come to some fence posts set in the hedge and continue straight ahead across the next two fields, still keeping a little to the right of the centre of the valley. There is a series of metal gates along this line.
In the third field, however, you take the lower and left-hand of the two gates facing you. The public

footpath continued beside a "No Trespassing" sign when we researched the walk – it should since have been removed. The path goes to the right of a tiny stream and a decaying area of bog woodland.

Keep to the right of the stream, slipping under a strand of barbed wire as you come close to some houses. This brings you on to the tarred road, and you turn left, passing the house named Distant Hills. Continue along the road, following the laurel hedge for a quarter of a mile.

The next buildings are Chalmington Farm, and you turn right after the first barn. This brings you through the centre of the farmyard and on to a muddy track that continues straight ahead into the fields. Towards the middle of the field you begin to head a little to the left of centre, bringing you to the remains of a gate in the hedgerow at the far end of the field.

Walk across the next two fields, to the gates facing you in each case, which brings you to a stream. The railway line is visible, about a quarter of a mile to your right.

Continue straight ahead across this field, which is arable after the lower boggy area, to the iron gate on the rise facing you, to the left of an electricity pole. This brings you into a trackway between double hedges, and this leads on to the tarred road. **Turn right, walk through Sandhills,**

and cross the railway bridge. On the other side there is a road junction. Here, to the left, a public trackway attractively fords the River Frome.

But you turn right, along the road signposted to "Evershot, Chelborough". Climb the hill, for just over a quarter of a mile, to the house near the top.

Turn right just before the house, following a wooden direction sign: "Bridleway Chantmarle 1". You walk along the drive towards Holway Farm, but only for 15 paces, and then turn left through a second iron gate. Walk up the slope, passing to the left of the farm buildings. Towards the top of the hill you pass an old chalkpit and then go through the iron gate facing you.

Turn immediately right and walk through the gap in the hedgerow into another field. Walk across a little left of centre, to the gap in the fence on the other side. You keep to about the same contour level, neither climbing further up the hill, nor drifting down the slope, but walking along it.

Head to the right of centre across the following field, to a wooden gate on the other side. Continue straight ahead across this field, for about 80 yards, to the gap with iron rails in the hedgerow facing you. From here the path follows the slope to the left of the farm, through an iron gate, and you cross the farm's access road.

On the other side there is a wooden gate, into a large arable field. The public footpath crosses through the middle of this, on a course that has been ploughed out. However, if you walk left of centre, and keep its higher hedgerow to your left, you can use the telegraph poles as indicators of general direction.

You should be heading for the left-hand and upper end of the main area of woodland, which has some distinctive fir trees, and lies just over a quarter of a mile away. You eventually follow the poles into the upper left-hand end of the field, beside the wood.

Enter the wood just to the left of the house, which stands down the slope on the other side of the trees. The path passes to the left of the house and becomes Robin Drive, with a mini zebra-crossing beside the line of garages.

At the end of Robin Drive you turn right along the tarred road, which is a public road passing through the Police Training College. The buildings are to the right and a car-park to the left. The buildings become progressively more interesting, culminating in the architectural splendour of Chantmarle.

The road from the Training College brings you to a lodge and road junction. Turn left here. You follow the lane for about half a mile, back into Frome St.Quintin to your car.

Chantmarle's history

Chantmarle, Dorset's Police Training College, is one of the finest country houses in the county. It dates from the 15th, 16th and early 17th centuries – with extensive additions westward that are more tasteful than average mid-1960s. The main block is as it was rebuilt by John Strode about 1612.

The outstanding feature from this period is the central porch, of three storeys, with its half-round oriel window set on moulded corbelling, with shell-head carvings on the niches below. The rich yellow stone came from the "Hamdon and Whetley" quarries, the best from Ham Hill (just over ten miles north-west) with the rubble coming from Whetley between Powerstock and Eggardon. ☐

Mappowder and Dorsetshire Gap

Distance: 7 miles.
Difficult bits: None.
State of paths: Damp throughout the winter but easy to find.
Scenery: Fine views from the open downs, contrasting with the wild, wooded and enclosed landscape below. The Dorsetshire Gap is a hub of ancient trackways, a mile from the nearest tarred road.
Historical interest: Mappowder Church; mediaeval Melcombe Park; Bronze Age burial mound; ancient trackways.
Natural history: Buzzards, more than on most of these walks; chalkland flora.
Literary associations: Theodore Powys, author of *Mr Weston's Good Wine,* lived in the village [1940-53] and is buried in the churchyard. The author and publisher Roland Gant has a cottage at Armswell Farm.

THIS WALK, of seven miles, is a pilgrimage to the centre of the county of Dorset — if you take the calculations in terms of its pre-1974 boundaries — where isolated deep-cut green lanes pass through a dip in the chalk hills. The trackways are ancient and the Dorsetshire Gap was the link between the prehistoric ridgeways of the Dorset Downs and the later droveways of the Blackmore Vale. Such is its remarkable atmosphere — which has to be experienced to be appreciated — that a visitors' book is kept in a biscuit tin at this remote crossroads. You normally have to climb a mountain to find that kind of facility.

The walk, which is mostly across unploughed pastures and between largish blocks of woodland, starts from Mappowder village. Mappowder lies in the vale midway between Piddletrenthide and Sturminster Newton.

Coming from the Piddle valley direction, you leave the B 3143 at Piddletrenthide and drive uphill along the lane signposted "Plush, Folly, Mappowder". Mappowder is five miles away.

Approaching by the Sturminster Newton route you turn off the A 357 at the western outskirts to the town (on the Newton side of the river) opposite the Red Lion. The road is signposted to Fifehead Neville and Hazelbury Bryan. In five miles, at Hazelbury Bryan, you pass the public house and climb uphill into the older part of the village. At the top of the slope you fork right along a side road that is signposted to Mappowder.

Park and start at Mappowder in the main street, called Hammond Street, which has the telephone kiosk, post office and church. There is room to pull off the road nearly opposite the church, and a few other wider points but take care not to block gateways.

Walk out of the village past the church. This is dedicated to Saints Peter and

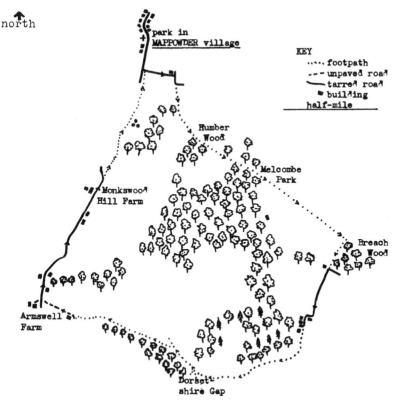

north

park in
MAPPOWDER village

Humber
Wood

Melcombe
Park

Monkswood
Hill Farm

Breach
Wood

Armswell
Farm

Dorset
shire Gap

Paul and was almost completely rebuilt in 1868 though it retains some earlier features, including a figurine of a crusader. This is in the wall, at the corner above the storage heater, on the right as you enter the building. It may mark a heart burial, of a knight who died overseas. The churchyard has the grave of Theodore Powys, the Dorset novelist, who died in 1953.

Continue out of the village in the direction of the hills. Twenty yards after the "Mappowder" village sign you turn left on to a short, straight, tarred farm road. It passes a farmyard at Mappowder Court and then bends to the right. A wooden signpost points to "Bridleway, Higher Melcombe". In about a hundred yards this road bends to the left and here you continue straight ahead, between double

hedges for a short way, and then follow the single hedgerow. You pass a small wood and follow a gate and stile into the next field.

Continue ahead, downhill, to a rather splendid wooden bridge, provided for riders and walkers, across a small stream. On the other side you climb the slope and then walk beside Humber Wood, keeping the trees to your right. Continue straight ahead after the wood, following the dense hedgerows of hawthorn and oaks up the slope. Keep on the lookout for roe deer. You enter a clump of oaks and the track descends to a stream that you step across.

On the other side, through an iron gate, you are in Melcombe Park, and cross another arm of the stream. At the top of the slope you come to an open

71

Mappowder's church is almost completely a Victorian restoration, of 1868. Theodore Powys, the Dorset novelist [1875-1953] is buried here. From 1940 he lived in the village, in the little lodge-like stone cottage that is overlooked by the church tower. Photograph: Colin Graham.

expanse of damp moorland, with a ruined house beyond. Do not walk on to the moorland, but turn left.

Ten paces to your left, in the hedge, is a wooden wicket gate. Go through this, into the field, but then turn immediately right, so that you are continuing to follow the hedgerow except on the other side.

Go through the iron gate at the end of the field. The hedgerow is riddled with burrows. At the other end of this field you go through another iron gate, a short distance to the left of the cattle trough.

Walk straight ahead across the next field into the far corner. Do not go through the iron gate facing you but turn to your right, through the remains of a wooden gate and into a wood. This brings you into an old, grassy cattle drove between the edge of the wood and the field. This used to be one of the major herding routes, for sheep and other stock between the central downlands and the market at Sturminster Newton. To your left is Breach wood.

At the end of the wood you pass some barns and continue straight ahead along a tarred road. Towards the end of this road you pass a bungalow and walk up to a brick and flint farmhouse. There is a notice: "No unauthorised vehicles beyond this point." Continue past the notice as although the public road ends here the concrete drive is a public bridleway. After the first two barns the farm road turns right, but you continue straight ahead, up a chalky slope.

At the top you take the right-hand of the set of three gates and continue around the back of the newest barn. This brings you to an arable field. The official route of the public bridleway is across the middle, but it is more considerate to follow the right-hand edge of the field. This is the route the local horseriders use and you get an extensive view over the adjoining woods.

At the end of the field there is a gate, which you ignore, and then a stile — which you cross. If you then walk up to the top of the Bronze Age burial mound to your left you will have a superb view over this scenic dip in the hills. The path continues ahead, along the edge of the ridge. It leads you down into a hollow way, and then two other hollow ways come together in turn. They look more like a collection of railway cuttings.

This is the Dorsetshire Gap. Beside a marker post, in an old biscuit tin in a plastic bag, is a visitors' book: "We, who have placed this book here for the interest of walkers, ask all who come, to respect the unique atmosphere of this ancient meeting-place of trackways, which has remained peaceful for centuries. By so doing, they will be showing their appreciation to the owner for access, besides helping to preserve an attractive part of our British heritage." The trackways here are smoothly engineered, with the one facing you (it comes from a hill-fort) having spoil used as banking. They appear neither to have evolved nor eroded into their present form, but to date from the time when the prehistoric forts were being constructed on these slopes. There is probably no better surviving example of a ridgeway junction and it is worth climbing to the top of the main hill for an overall look. An excavation is needed to find whether there is an Iron Age turf-line beneath the embanked section of track.

The walk continues to the right (right, that is, from your original entry into the Gap) and you descend to the foot of an ash wood into a field. Go through the iron gate and then turn left, to follow the edge of the wood. Go through the gate into the next field, but then continue straight ahead, ignoring the track that turns into the wood. You slip under the wire and keep following the outside of the wood. Aim for a large asbestos barn, in front of you, when it comes into sight.

The path now follows some oak trees, at the foot of the main slope, and leads you to an iron gate. When you come to the barn you join a farm track and follow it to the road at Armswell Farm.

Turn right and follow the tarred road, past Lovelace Copse and Woodlands Farm. In just over half a mile, around the bend at the top of the rise, are some barns and a bungalow and then the main buildings of Monkwood Hill Farm.

A hundred yards after the farm you fork off the tarred road and continue straight ahead, through the gate facing you. You go through a gap in the hedge on the other side of the field and then follow the left-hand hedgerow, around a wet area, to the corner of the field by the wood.

Slip under the wire into the next field. There are the remains of an old stile in the hedgerow, but no longer in any condition to be used. Walk across the centre of the field.

To the left of the gas pumping station you'll see a modern stile. Cross this and walk beside the compound fence. At the other side you go through the wooden farm gate (not the smaller wire gate) and cross the field to a stile in the corner facing you.

Then climb the slope to a black painted gate beside a cattle trough. Turn left along the drive and walk down on to the lane. Turn right and you are now back in Mappowder. □

Evershot
and
Melbury

Distance: 7 miles.
Difficult bits: A stream to cross, so pick a dry time of the year.
State of paths: Muddy in parts.
Scenery: Lush and pastoral, typical of west Dorset, with glimpses of the hills and a fine country house and its park. Melbury Osmond is a delightful stone and thatch village with some magnificent trees.
Historical interest: Melbury House; Lion Gate; Evershot church.
Natural history: Wild roe deer if you are lucky, and deer park Sika and other species guaranteed; buzzards; wide variety of wild flowers.

THIS IS an unusual *seven* mile walk through parkland with fine trees, architectural gems, and even herds of red, fallow and Japanese sika deer. Then there is the appeal of being able to walk through the heart of one of the greatest private estates in Dorset.   In the first section of the walk there are a couple of obstructions to overcome but there are no other difficulties and most of the going is easy. The walk drops from a 700 foot hill to valley bogs and winter conditions will call for rough clothing and gumboots. But there are no problems after Melbury Osmond as you walk on the luxury surface of an estate drive. Evershot, where the walk starts, is reached from the A37 (Dorchester-Yeovil road) a mile west of Holywell which lies at the foot of a long hill where the main road drops from the Dorset Downs.

Park on the verge at the crossroads on top of the hill half a mile west of Evershot on the road to Beaminster. This hill is a continuation of Evershot's principal street.

Walk along the road north from the crossroads and signposted "Girt Farm Only." Follow tarred road where it swings left at another sign "Girt Farm". You are now at a height of 730 feet and there is a fine view of the hills above Halstock and then leftward into west Dorset. The hill in the centre of the middle distance, looking like the hull of an upturned boat, is the motte and bailey of Castle Hill at East Chelborough. Buzzards were circling and mewing over this valley in August.

Keep straight on the tarred road to Girt Farm (girt is a Dorset dialect word for 'great'). **Take the track**

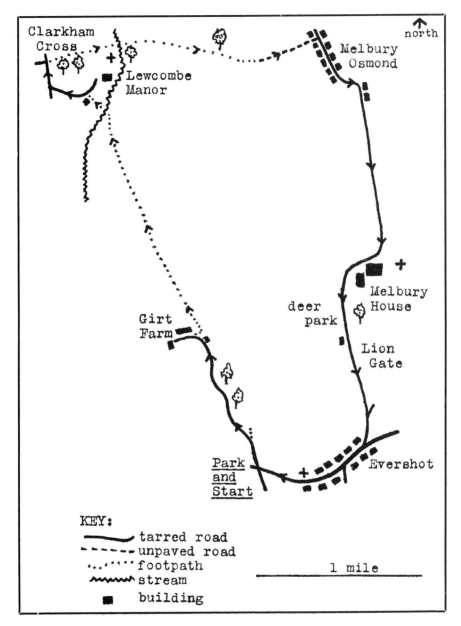

KEY:

———— tarred road
– – – – unpaved road
·····'''' footpath
∿∿∿ stream
■ building

1 mile

that leads right from the farm buildings and turn almost immediately left to follow the park fence. Follow tractor marks across the field and keep the park fence on your right. The next section is better marked as a rough track runs beside the iron railings.

Melbury – one of the great houses of
Dorset – belittles its private church.

**Turn right across the middle of the
field at the muddy area where you
leave the corner of the park fence.
Go through the first gate and head
left towards the gate in the middle
of the hedge at the bottom end of
the next field.**

This gate is between old oak trees
at the lowest point of the field.

**Cross the field ahead along the
tractor marks and you will find a
bog crossed by concrete slats and
railway sleepers where you enter the**
**next field. Continue straight across
an open ditch and follow to the
right of the hedgerow facing you.**
This adjoining field juts into the
one where you are walking. At the
end of this length of hedgerow (as
far as you can go) there is a gate
and a track runs through it.

**Head diagonally right across this
field which is flatter.** Go through into the next field where you pass
above a tributary of the River Yeo.
Keep this on your left and you will
soon see Lewcombe Manor and its
copper beech tree overlooking you.
The left corner of this field is above
the stream which lies in a deep cut-

76

ting. The right corner has a tall oak. **Midway along, 20 paces from the large oak, there is a gap in the hedge and when we prepared the walk there was an awkward fence to climb.** Things may have improved.

Turn right along the stream bank to the corner. Cross onto the stones opposite. In summer you can do this and keep dry but in winter you may get both feet wet. But the stream bed is comprised of stones at this point and there is no danger of you sinking if you have to step across.

Head up the hill (keeping Lewcombe Manor on your right).

Cross into the next field at the remains of a blue gate under an ash tree and head for the fence just to the right of the house with a tiled roof. Leave the field at the left corner, by the house, where some lengths of timber are a further unfortunate obstruction.

Go left along the tarred road. Cross the cattle grid at the manor gates and turn right on to the tarred road. Turn right at the signposted Clarkham Cross down an old green lane which runs between a red iron barn and a wood. This lane has an extraordinary variety of species of wild flowers. Carry straight on where the track becomes narrower. **Go through the right-hand gate at the end and continue ahead beside the left hedgerow.** The track resumes at the end of the field and drops into a hollow.

The next gate is at an old humped bridge. Lewcombe church can be seen through the trees on the right. The path climbs up through a wood. **At the top of the wood cross the field diagonally in a right-hand direction, following a trodden path.** There is a gate at the far end of the field by an adjoining overgrown field.

Open this gate (it opens, just) but don't stray into the overgrown field where there is another gate (which doesn't open). Follow the left hedgerow. This path becomes a dirt track which later turns green but is easy to follow, with a hedge on the left and a fence to the right. This becomes a lane that brings you into Melbury Osmond at the tarred road.

Turn right and walk down through the village. At the end of the road, after two corners, you enter the parkland that surrounds Melbury House. You are allowed to do so!

Carry straight on. The public path is the tarred drive that crosses Melbury Park and passes its sheep herds. Keep straight on to Melbury House where the road bends sharply right. Melbury House is the seat of the Strangways family and one of the greatest country houses in Dorset. The church lies below it, down the hill, and the tower that stands above the house itself was built by Sir Giles Strangways shortly before 1540.

At the next corner the drive goes over a long cattle grid and enters a park with red, sika and fallow deer. It is one of the few deerparks in Britain with three species. Keep to the tarred drive through the deer park and you leave Melbury Park through Lion Gate — 17th century rusticated gate-piers surmounted by lions — and continue until you are in Evershot.

Turn right at the main road and walk up the village street. There are raised pavements between lines of town-like old houses. The church stands at the top end of the street and you climb to the top of the hill where you will see your car ☐

Halstock and West Chelborough

Distance: 5 miles.

Difficult bits: None.

State of paths: The usual qualification on vale walking – damp for most of the year.

Scenery: The line of wooded hills along the Somerset border, upstream of the lake at Sutton Bingham, with mediaeval tracks, Roman villa and cul-de-sac hamlets.

Historical interest: Halstock's Roman villa; Court Farm mediaeval moat; St Andrew's church, West Chelborough.

Natural history: Deer country; skeins of duck; a generally enhanced bird-list because of the proximity of Sutton Bingham lake; foxes and badgers.

UNDULATING, WELL-WOODED country-side covers the Dorset side of the large lake at Sutton Bingham, three miles south of Yeovil. The *five* mile walk starts from the Dorset village of Halstock, tramps along two miles of completely unmodernised mediaeval road, and then crosses a varied tract of land to the dead-end hilltop hamlet of West Chelborough.

Remarkably, the green lane out from Halstock runs over the foundations of an extensive Roman Villa. Finds are in Dorset County Museum, Dorchester. The track coincides with the original entrance to the villa, which may be more than coincidence.

As for walking conditions, these can be changeable. When there is no longer drought you will need waterproof footwear as this land can be as moist as any in Dorset. Only in a couple of places is the path narrow and hemmed in by vegetation and the walk does not otherwise require any effort. It has no steep slopes.

For a picnic afterwards nowhere can better the mile-and-a-half of open reservoir water at Sutton Bingham where, in a knob of land between two arms of the lake, there is one of the finest, simplistic churches in these parts. It still has its ancient wall paintings. Drinking walkers will spot a pub en route (the Fox at Corscombe) and another, the Quiet Woman, is by the Halstock starting point.

The main road turning to Halstock is off the A37 Dorchester to Yeovil road, 16 miles north of Dorchester. It is signposted "Closworth ½, Halstock 2¼" and is just north of where you pass the Somerset boundary sign.

On entering Halstock village, turn right after the Quiet Woman inn, and park somewhere close to the tri-

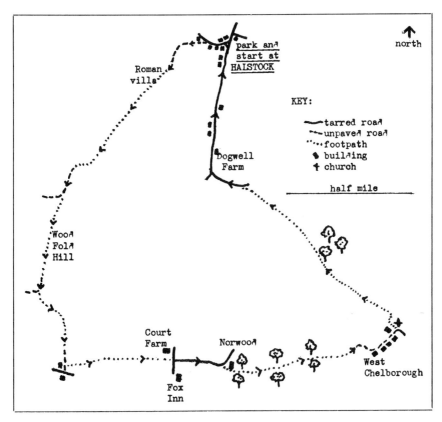

north

park and start at HALSTOCK

Roman villa

Dogwell Farm

Wood Fold Hill

Court Farm

Norwood

Fox Inn

West Chelborough

angle of grass facing E. J. Salter's village stores. Park considerately here, leaving your car in one of the wider stretches of road. If there is a shortage of space you can turn back towards the Quiet Woman and park on the wide grass verge on the left. **Walk along the road signposted to "Cheddington, South Perrott" for about a hundred yards.** On going round the first bend you face a white-painted three-storey house called New Inn Farm.

Fork left here, beside the left-hand side of the house, along a rough track. As the track climbs a slope, after about half-a-mile, it crosses the foundations of Roman walls and courtyards. These are part of an ex-tensive villa site covering two acres which was systematically excavated in the 1970s when work spread from the fields on either side into the track itself, and only two inches under the surface of the old road there are the limestone bases of thick walls which were apparently the gateway into the building.

Parts of this walling were exposed in the 1970s. The villa was occupied throughout the Roman period from the 1st to 4th centuries and almost certainly lies on the site of an earlier, Iron Age, farmstead. After the build-ing footings, beside an oak tree, there is a Roman well which is still conveniently supplying water.

79

Villa rooms with underfloor heating.

Shortly after the villa remains the track narrows to a pleasant footpath running between densely overgrown hedgerows and coppiced hazel. In a mile the track becomes wider again and climbs a rise. At the top there is a second track forking to the right. Make sure you ignore this and continue straight ahead downhill. The track then climbs again, on to Wood Fold Hill.

At the foot of this hill you ignore the main track, which veers to the right, and again make sure that you continue straight ahead, along a grassier lane. You pass a small sewerage plant with its own gurgling stream of 'treated' brown effluent which you can later go home and drink as it drains into Sutton Bingham reservoir.

Forty yards from the end of the lane, as you reach a house and can see the tarred road, there is a wooden gate into the field on the left. Go through this and walk downhill to the bottom right-hand corner of the field. Here there are some old fence posts and you slip through a hole in the hedgerow to the other side. Walk across the corner of this arable field, for about twenty yards, to the remains of a stone stile.

You now follow the right-hand hedgerow, aiming for the gate in the distance midway between Court Farm and the Fox Inn. Walk past the garden wall between the staddle stones of Court Farm — the large stone mullioned farmhouse on the left — and on to the tarred road. A square of ponds and bogs surround Court Farm and form the outline of a mediaeval moat dating from the time when this spot was monastic and the site of Abbey Grange.

Go straight across the road, into the tarred lane with a "no through road" sign. In about 500 yards you come to Norwood Cottage, a slate-roofed house with dormer-windows.

Leave the tarred road here and walk beside the right-hand wall of the cottage. At the end of the garden the public path goes through a wooden gate into a wood. The track runs straight ahead through the wood, for a hundred yards, to another gate.

Walk straight ahead across the arable field, and through a hunting gate into the wood on the other side (the gate is about thirty yards to the left of an electricity pole). At the end of the narrow belt of trees the path again continues straight ahead across an arable field and enters the next wood, again a few feet to the left of the power line.

Walk ahead through the trees along the grass covered track to another hunting gate. This next field is grass and you walk up to an iron gate in the top right-hand corner. Follow the right-hand fence across the next pasture and leave by an iron gate in the corner, which is once more beside an electricity pole.

You now follow the dirt track uphill and keep on it across the con- creted cow-yard of **Manor Farm** to the houses of **West Chelborough.** The view from here carries you across the wooded belt of hills along the Somerset border to the distant shapes of Exmoor on the left and the Mendips on the right. As the track becomes tarred you pass a farmhouse and come to the almost-dainty church of St Andrew, newly reroofed with stone slates and saved from the prospect of becoming a ruin.

Between the farmhouse and the church hedge there is a dirt track. This takes you round a corner to an iron gate. Do not go through the gate but turn left along a narrow path between two hedgerows. After about a hundred yards the path narrows but you still continue along it as it is walkable. It runs through lush vegetation for a few hundred yards and then emerges abruptly into a field at a point where there used to be a gate. Cross the wire here (it is low enough to step over) and continue ahead across the centre of the next two fields.

Head towards the left-hand end of the wood. This is facing you at the bottom of the gentle slope. Beside the left-hand corner of the wood there is a wooden gate and a bridge of railway sleepers over a stream.

Cross this and continue straight ahead, uphill along the left-hand side of the wood. There is a string of badger setts above the track. At the end of the trees the track continues ahead between two hedgerows. This is an old cattle drove which in a mile comes out on to a tarred road.

Turn left along this road. In about 150 yards you come to a junction with another tarred road. Here you turn right and walk back into Halstock to your car. □

Melbury Bubb

Distance: 5 miles.

Difficult bits: The tricky moment is crossing the A37 on a blind bend – keep listening and on no account linger in the road.

State of paths: Generally good, despite some coming and going across the spring line.

Scenery: Well-wooded walking country on a northern spur of the Dorset Downs, with excellent views across the Blackmore Vale.

Historical interest: Farm granary on staddle stones; limekiln; manor house; Melbury Bubb church; remarkable Saxon carving turned upside down and reused as a font; table tombs; mediaeval cross base; Melbury Park lodge; turnpike milestone.

Natural history: Typical buzzard and roe deer country, with both in quantity.

Literary associations: The countryside that was the setting for Thomas Hardy's novel *The Woodlanders*.

DORSET'S FINEST walking country is undoubtedly its chalk downs, but to put scale into the heights and produce something dramatic and varied you have to look to the slopelands where the escarpment breaks into wooded hills and valleys. This five mile walk crosses the northern fringes of the Dorset Downs beside the main A37 Dorchester to Yeovil road, 13 miles north-west of Dorchester. It is a landscape more visited as an entity in Edwardian times because Bubb Down Hill was one of the ac-claimed viewpoints of Dorset and the parkland surroundings had been romanticised by Hardy in "The Woodlanders". The walk offers beech wood hangers on the steep slopes, ancient trackways, and a gem of a church in the cul-de-sac village of Melbury Bubb.

Park and start in a layby with a 'P' sign on the west side of Bubb Down Hill on the A37 just over a mile north of the turn-off to Evershot which is at the foot of a wide three-lane highway which sweeps down

The A37: park on the slope of Bubb Down Hill.

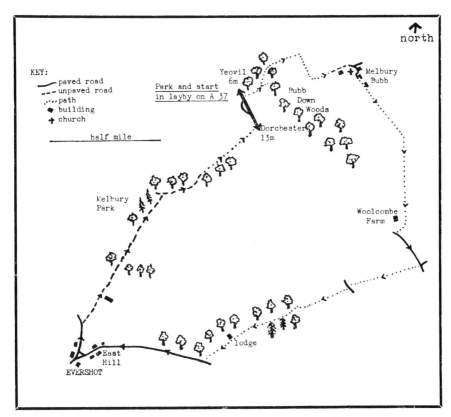

north

Yeovil
6m

Park and start
in layby on A 37

Bubb
Down
Woods

Melbury
Bubb

Dorchester
13m

Melbury
Park

Woolcombe
Farm

lodge

East
Hill
EVERSHOT

the side of the downs after Clay Pigeon Restaurant. The layby on Bubb Down Hill has open views to the west, to Melbury Park and house, and a field rising into a wooded hillside on the other side of the road. If you approach from the Yeovil direction, it lies a mile-and-a-half from the Melbury Osmond turn-off, on the rising ground after the two turn-offs to Stockwood and Chetnole.

Walk downhill to the lower end of the layby, cross the road, and go about 50 paces to the gate beside the wood. Turn right through this. Walk up the slope, with the trees to your left.

The track runs into the wood and then forks left, along the lower of the two paths. This curves around the hillside, through the trees, to an iron gate with the entire spread of the Blackmore Vale visible behind. **Go through the gate and walk straight ahead across the field.** There is a cattle trough to your right, and you walk downhill towards an Ordnance Survey concrete instrument pillar. Behind it is a hedgerow.

Turn right along this hedge and follow it downhill to an iron gate in the corner of the field. You are looking down, through the hedge, at the manor house and church of Melbury Bubb.

Go through the gate and walk straight ahead for about 40 paces, and then turn to the left and walk downhill to the wooden gate and

83

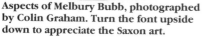

Aspects of Melbury Bubb, photographed by Colin Graham. Turn the font upside down to appreciate the Saxon art.

barns. There is a limekiln in the chalkpit to your left. The track passes through the farmyard, beside a shed on staddle stones, and then follows the manor house wall. Turn the corner and the gate to the church is on your right. The churchyard is a pleasant diversion as it contains an attractive collection of large yellow-stone table tombs from the 17th century. Inside the church there is part of the shaft of a Saxon stone cross, circled with a limestone relief of hounds snarling at a stag at bay. One dog has a hare in its mouth, and another what looks to be a smaller dog—dog eats dog. There is also a dolphin-like sea creature and six snake-head coils. The basis of the church building is 15th century, via an almost complete reconstruction in 1851. Outside the porch, behind the main cluster of five tombs, there is the square base of a mediaeval cross.

On leaving the churchyard you turn right at the junction, beside the post

box, and walk to Bubb Down Farm at the end of the lane. Continue straight ahead through the farmyard, along a track signposted "Footpath Woolcombe 1". Follow the right-hand hedgerow to the end corner of the first field and then continue straight ahead across the next, to a couple of fence bars in the hedge facing you. Walk straight ahead across the next field. Although there is no path that can be seen on the ground, you will not go astray as long as you keep the buildings of Melbury Bubb in a direct line behind your back. At the left end of the field there is a railway line (Bristol to Weymouth) and at the right-hand end there is a wood. There were four buzzards soaring and mewing over the wood the day we researched the walk. As you cross the top of the rise in the middle of the field the railway line is embanked and clearly in view.

Turn slightly leftward down the slope in the direction of the thatched farmhouse standing beside the line about a mile away. You come to the beginning of a farm track between two electric fences.

This track leads to Woolcombe Farm, a large slate-roofed building beneath an escarpment of the Dorset Downs. The track passes the wall of the farmhouse garden and emerges on a tarred road.

Turn left, for about 200 yards, to a fork on the other side of the dip. Here you turn to the right (beside the "no through road" sign) and walk into a pronounced depression which marks the course of an ancient horse-road. As you turn through the bushes into this track, beware of a strand of eye-level barbed wire. The track runs uphill for half-a-mile in a straight line, running along a hollow between a bank to the left and a fence on the right. The undergrowth is patchy and can be skirted without much trouble.

At the top of the hill the track drops down on to the main road. Cross the road and climb the bank on the other side, a few feet to the left of the point immediately opposite. There is a gap in the vegetation on the slope. But make sure you do not linger in the road as traffic sweeps round the curve of the hill at speed.

At the top of the bank you slip under an electric fence and into the field.

Follow the right-hand hedgerow to the wood, about 200 yards away. Just before you reach the wood, in the corner of the field, there is a double iron gate. Cross this and then continue ahead, on your previous course, into the trees.

Here you resume walking along a sunken trackway which bends slightly to the left and then runs downhill through the trees in a straight line. As you come to the edge of the wood you see an arable field.

From here the path follows the edge of the wood, with the trees to your right and the field on the left, and passes beside an 1859 lodge at one of the entrances to Melbury Park. The path comes out at a tarred road. **Turn right and walk into Evershot, which is half-a-mile away.** In the village, at the bottom of East Hill, there is a triangle of grass with a tall holm oak at the centre. This is known as The Common.

Turn right here and walk along the tarred road signposted "Public footpath only. No vehicles". About 150 yards along this road there is a gate across it (usually open) and a rough track forks to the right. Turn right along this track and walk uphill. You pass a Victorian house with high chimney stacks. On this track in February we found a squashed frog. It was not quite a conventional first sign of spring, but it must have meant something. From the top of the hill the track drops into a park style landscape of trees and fields. Your car is visible on the hillside in the middle distance.

Walk down the stony track to the foot of the hill. At the bottom there is a junction with another track, and you turn right. This track leads you towards the rumble of main road traffic. After passing a wood to the left of the track, it goes through a short belt of trees, and then climbs a field, with the wood now to your right. At the end of the wood there is a gate and you go through this and continue straight ahead. Walk uphill to the cattle grid and gate in the fence, on to the main road.

Turn left. You pass a milestone—"6 Maiden Newton, 7 Yeovil"—and your car is 300 yards away. □

Opposite: manhole at Evershot covering the source of the River Frome. Above: trees, thatch and the church at the top end of Evershot's town-like village street. Photographs: Colin Graham.

Nether Compton and the Butterfly Farm

Distance: 5 miles.

Difficult bits: A summertime disadvantage of undergrowth and a winter problem with the wet – wear rough clothing and gumboots, and even take a pair of secetures.

State of paths: Well marked and easy to find but with the tendency as mentioned above to either fill up with flora or water.

Scenery: Deep-cut lanes through yellow cliffs in a belt of sandy hills with fine views over the Blackmore and Somerset vales. The most fertile soil in the county.

Historical interest: Nether Compton church; ancient hollow-ways; Stallen limekiln; mediaeval strip lynchets; crenellated lodge; Compton House.

Natural history: Widely varied range of wild flowers; woodpeckers; sand martins; owls; roe deer; Butterfly Farm.

NETHER COMPTON is an attractive culdesac village two miles north-west of Sherborne. This *five* mile walk explores some of its extensive network of deeply-gouged lanes and trackways that cut through the hills. The green lanes of this parish are amongst the best preserved in the whole of Dorset, with ancient hedgerows left intact and the surfaces free from obstacles and obstructions. Several are not shown on the maps as they are in a different legal class from most rights-of-way, being public unclassified county roads. They are in regular use by local people, and on the day we researched the route we came across more than thirty people on foot and horseback. This was a record number for any Dorset walk that is away from the coast, and does not include any of the visitors at the Compton House butterfly farm. That's also on offer, as the right-of-way brings you almost to its back-door, so make sure you have a little cash in your pocket.

To find Nether Compton you take the A30 dual-carriageway between Sherborne and Yeovil. Turn north from the main road at the valley dip about a mile-and-a-half from Sherborne. The signpost points to "Nether Compton $1\frac{1}{4}$".

Park in the village street. The road is wide, both before the church, and after it towards the Yeovil turning.

Begin the walk by continuing along the street. After the telephone kiosk there is a "No through road" sign and you walk along this road in the direction of the Griffin's Head public house.

At this corner you follow the road, and the stream, around to the right. Keep following the tarred road and the stream, passing old cottages and barns and then some more recent development, and Folly Cottage. This cottage marks the end of the village and the road is now unpaved. At times, however, it can still double as a stream bed. It skirts the foot of a hill and gradually edges towards the head

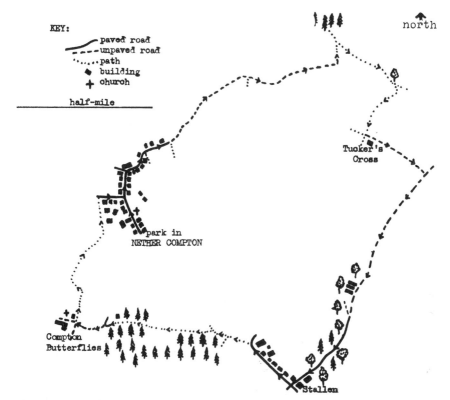

KEY:

⟋ paved road
- - - unpaved road
٠٠٠٠٠ path
◆ building
✚ church

half-mile

Tucker's
Cross

park in
NETHER COMPTON

Compton
Butterflies

Stallen

of the valley, over the course of about a mile.

Continue along this main track, which is hedged on each side, for its entirety. Near the end, it suddenly bends to the left, and brings you down to a stream, beneath a line of electricity cables.

Here the stub of the track turns left, towards a small spruce wood, but you turn right, through an iron gate, and follow the stream bed to the top of the valley. Near the top, on your right, you pass an exposed cliff-face of Yeovil sands with alternate bands of stone. It is about twenty feet high, with sand martin holes and owl pellets beneath the ivy overhang. At the foot, the sand is bloodstained by a layer of gory dew, a moss-like micro-plant.

At the top of the field you go through a gate into a small beech glade, smothered in foxgloves. **Near the top the track forks and you take the right-hand alternative.** This brings you into a narrow, double hedged path, with distant views over the surrounding countryside. It leads to a corrugated iron barn, at Tucker's Cross, and here you turn left.

A farm road runs in a straight line for about a third of a mile. Turn right at the end, along another farm track that slowly descends towards the distant hum of main road traffic. You look across the western parts of the Blackmore Vale. Some of these fields on the Yeovil sands, amongst the most easily cultivated and highest natural fertility of all Dorset land, are used in the production of turf for suburban lawns. A small belt of woodland discreetly hides the extensive build-

Above: Nether Compton church with the lightest of four o'clock shadows. Opposite: Compton House, the Goodden family pile, now conceals the internal jungle – the habitat for Worldwide Butterflies. Photographs: Colin Graham.

ings and slurry lagoons of a battery farm system. The track is then tarred and overlooks, through the trees, the hamlet of Stallen. Finally, the road drops down between high sandy cliffs to the cottages below.

Turn right at the crossroads and walk along the road, passing the houses and farmyard to the sharp bend at the imposing house at the corner. Here you pass an electricity junction-box and continue straight ahead, along a double hedged dirt track. At the top of the slope it turns into a wood, but you continue straight ahead, downhill, into another lane cut through the yellow cliffs. On your right there is a large opening, with the remains of a door and a recess inside with a well-built stone arch. Further along is another opening. It looks like a lime-kiln.

After the hollow, about thirty yards beyond this second opening, you turn left through the iron gate facing you. This path skirts a larch plantation, and then continues straight ahead through the iron gate in front of you. You then walk beside a mediaeval cultivation terrace, to the belt of trees on the other side of the field.

Here there is another gate and the path continues straight ahead through the wood. To your right is an elegantly crenallated lodge. You then descend to a tarred driveway and turn left along it, for about a hundred yards.

Then you continue straight ahead, through an iron gate, along a back entrance to Compton House and church. The house — which is impressive though largely Victorian — is opened to the public. It is the ancestral home of Robert Goodden, whose family memorials are in the nearby church, and provides the counterpoint for his simulated jungle of Worldwide Butterflies. There is also a silk farm. An admission charge is made, but it is a worthwhile diversion, particularly as you have no worries about parking the car!

The footpath turns right as you approach the house, through a black-painted metal gate beside a barn. This is signposted: "Footpath, Nether Compton ½".

At the other side of the field, beyond a beech clump, is another metal gate and the path crosses an arable field. It would show consideration, and also makes the going easier, to walk around the left-hand edge. At the bottom of the field you come to a stream and turn left, towards the bungalows. There is a stile on to the road, just beyond the iron gate.

Turn right along the road, into Nether Compton. At the road junction, by the telephone kiosk, you turn right and walk back to your car. ☐

Poyntington and Holway

Distance: 6 miles.
Difficult bits: None.
State of paths: Muddy except in high summer.
Scenery: Ridge of attractive limestone downland between the Dorset and Somerset vales to the north of Sherborne. There are wide views across the flatlands.
Historical interest: Holway hamlet; turnpike toll house; Poyntington church and effigy.
Natural history: Buzzard, fox, badger and roe deer country yet again — but they are the delights of exploring Dorset's deep-cut valleys.
Literary associations: The Court House, next to Poyntington church, is the home of the historical novelist Rachel Billington.

IF IT is possible these days to regard anywhere in Dorset as little known and neglected, perhaps the phrase can still apply to the pocket of limestone uplands north of Sherborne. The parishes of Poyntington and Sandford Orcas were taken from Somerset in 1896 and the gap between them, the hamlet of Holway, was brought into Dorset to tidy the boundary in the 1960s. Geologically, the ground is constantly changing from stone to sand and clay, and with it the vegetation and scenery. Springs on the downland north of Poyntington are the source of the River Yeo. This six mile walk is mainly across easy ground, though with some steeper slopes, but the muddy patches make rubber boots essential.

Park and start in the centre of Poyntington village. Poyntington is signposted north from the A30 road, a mile east of Sherborne, at the village of Oborne. In the middle of Poyntington there is a wide triangle of tarmac with a signpost standing at the centre — pointing to Oborne and Sherborne in one direction, and Sandford Orcas and Corton Denham in the other.

On leaving your car, walk down the third tarred road, the one without any direction pointer. You pass the telephone box and a line of chained staddle stones. On the left there is a thicket of bamboo, and you then walk beside a stream. As the stream flows to the right, into a garden, there is a staggered road junction.

Take the second turning on the left, next to a no-through-road sign. This road climbs the hill and passes to the left of a white-painted stone and tile cottage. Immediately after the cottage, the road becomes a dirt track and it winds up the hill.

At the top there is a short level stretch. Here you turn sharply to the left, making sure you do so before the track forks in two direc-

tions, and walk up to a wooden gate. If you go too far, you will see a wooden signpost saying: "Bridleway, Poyntington Hill". This points you back to the gate.

Once through the gate, you follow the right-hand hedgerow, with the view of the village and valley to your left. The stone bank, with the hedge, is the county boundary with Somerset but until the changes it only marked a parish division. After about three-quarters of a mile you come to the end of the field. A hundred yards before this you turn to the left and descend the hill, into a projecting piece of natural downland which lies between two fields.

There is a wooden gate near the left-hand corner and you go through this, and walk downhill along a wide, damp cattle-drove to the stream and road. Cross the road into the field opposite. This path is signposted "Bridleway, Wheat Sheaf Hill" and follows the left-hand hedgerow, beside a stream bed. This land used to be part of the Tenant's Cow Down, a block of common land covering more than a hundred acres. At the end of the field, by a hollow with a spring, you go through a gate and continue to follow the edge of the stream bed.

In about 200 yards there is a brick-arched bridge, under a roadway. Go through this. The day we researched the walk it was providing cover for an old wooden farm-cart, carrying the name "S. W. Dare, Wickham House, Marston Magna". On the other side of the bridge you come to a road junction. There is a signpost: "Sherborne 3¼".

Do not take this road but continue straight ahead, along the tarred road beside the post box, and downhill. At the foot of the hill turn left along the road signposted "Holway, Sandford Orcas". As you go down this

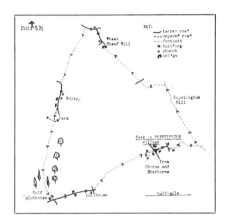

hill, round the bend, a line of poles begins. Between the fourth and fifth telegraph pole, on the left, there is a wooden gate.

Go through this and walk straight ahead, across the field to the gate in the hedge opposite. In only about 20 paces there is another gate facing you. Open this and follow the left-hand hedgerow, walking under a power line. In the next field you follow the right-hand hedgerow, and you continue to follow the line of fields at the foot of a steep ridge.

In the right-hand corner of the field just after another line of electricity poles, there is a gate. The next section of path is a well-defined terrace and follows the left-hand hedge, passing an oak tree. You emerge on a tarred road.

Continue straight ahead, uphill, and walk through the hamlet of Holway. As you come to the end of the line of stone farm buildings on the right-hand side of the road, at the corner, there is a signpost: "Bridleway, Higher Sandford".

You take this farm track and continue straight ahead. At the farmyard, in only about 100 yards, the track splits to the left and right.

Again you continue straight ahead,

Poyntington church and one of its residents (opposite). The building on the other page is a turnpike tollhouse, up on the hills. Photographs: Colin Graham.

through the right-hand of the two metal gates facing you. This track bends a little to the right at the foot of the slope, beside a heap of stones strewn with ammonite fossils, and then follows the left-hand hedgerow towards the centre of the wooded hills in front of you. You pass a cattle trough and shortly after this the hedge ends. There is a single oak tree and beyond it a broad expanse of grassland. Keep walking straight ahead to the plantation facing you. There is a slight dip in the hills at this point with a small patch of grass visible at the top. You may see distant figures crossing the skyline here as there is a golf course on top of the hill. The foot of this range of hills used to be the ancient, and naturally-defined, border between Somerset and Dorset.

To the right of an ash tree and a stand of poplars there is a gate into the wood. This plantation is unusual in being almost wholly comprised of cupressus, the quick-growing evergreen that has become boringly popular for suburban hedging. **Climb up the firebreak to the top of the hill, passing a corrugated iron hut.** You are now on Sherborne golf course, scenically magnificent at the top of the hills above Sandford Orcas, its views covering the flatlands of Somerset.

Continue walking ahead, aiming for the building on the skyline, and walk between the club-house and the golf shop. Walk out through the white-painted gates on to the tarred road at Clatcombe Cross.

Turn left. The road passes through a farm and on to a crossroads at the main road. Here there is a turn-pike tollhouse.

Cross over, on to the road signposted to Oborne, but only follow it for about ten paces. You go through the fence into the field on your left. Walk diagonally across this field to the opposite corner where you will find the remains of an old stone stile in the hedge.

Cross to the other side of the hedge and turn right, walking at the edge of the field with the hedge-row on your right.

At the top, on the skyline, you find a gap in the hedge. From here you can look across the valley, in front of you, to Poyntington village and the hillside opposite where you walked earlier.

Walk downhill, in a straight line, aiming for the cedar tree to the left of the house beside Poyntington church. As you come closer to the tree you will see, to the right of it, a wooden gate and a tarred drive leading down the slope to your car. On the right, about 30 yards after the gate, there is a path to the church, which despite 1863 rebuilding has an attractive tower and a knight effigy. ☐

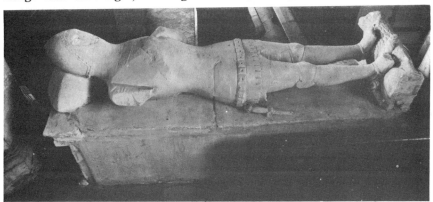

Park considerately.
Take only photographs.
Leave only footprints.
Shut the gates.

— the country code
that doesn't sound
as if it has been
written by a committee